TEXTS AND STUDIES

CONTRIBUTIONS TO

BIBLICAL AND PATRISTIC LITERATURE

EDITED BY

J. ARMITAGE ROBINSON D.D.

HON. PH.D. GÖTTINGEN HON. D.D. HALLE

CANON OF WESTMINSTER

VOL. VII.

No. 1. THE MEANING OF HOMOOUSIOS IN THE 'CONSTANTINOPOLITAN' CREED

THE MEANING OF HOMOOUSIOS

IN THE

'CONSTANTINOPOLITAN' CREED

BY

J. F. BETHUNE-BAKER B.D.

FELLOW AND DEAN OF PEMBROKE COLLEGE CAMBRIDGE

Wipf & Stock
PUBLISHERS
Eugene, Oregon

Wipf and Stock Publishers
199 W 8th Ave, Suite 3
Eugene, OR 97401

The Meaning of Homoousios in the 'Constantinopolitan' Creed
By Bethune-Baker, J.R.
ISBN: 1-59244-898-4
Publication date 9/29/2004
Previously published by Cambridge, 1901

CONTENTS.

ADDITIONAL NOTES.

Introductory.

THE history of the Arian controversy has often been written. And whoever has essayed the difficult task has, of course, been obliged to investigate more or less carefully the history of the various watch-words and rallying-cries of parties in the long impassioned struggle. The sympathies of historians have naturally been enlisted on one side or on the other, consciously or unconsciously, from the day on which immediately after the Council of Nicaea Eusebius penned his *Apologia* to his people of Caesarea[1] for his own acceptance of a formula which differed in some important respects from the Creed in which he and they had been baptized. And the technical terms which were used, the various definitions or descriptions of the Faith which were offered, have not always been explained alike. At least their full significance—in view of their original meaning and history—has not always been drawn out. Yet with regard to the final issue of the controversy there has been, it seems, all through the centuries, complete unanimity among all writers. The settled historical tradition has been that after all the changes and chances of more than half a century the definition of the Faith which was agreed to at Nicaea was reaffirmed in all essentials by the Council of Constantinople. The Church was never Arian; never really semi-Arian in heart or mind; but at the time of the Council of Nicaea the real drift of Arian teaching and the inevitable consequences of Arian methods of reasoning and interpretation—and the utter hopelessness of attempts at compromise with Arian principles—were understood by few. The real issues were clearly

[1] Socr. *H. E.* i 8.

seen only by a very small minority of the bishops and others who were present; and had the Arians 'managed' their case a little more cleverly—had they been a little less outspoken or a little less openly subtle in their interpretation of the various scriptural phrases which were suggested as sufficient description of the common faith, they might have secured from the Council such a Creed as they themselves could readily have signed. But the clumsiness or the honesty of the Arians, and the insight and persistence of the small minority—who represented little more than Alexandria and the Church of the West—forced on the great majority of Eastern bishops the acceptance of a technical term which they did not like and only partly understood. It was only a grudging consent that they gave at the time to the Creed. It served the need of the moment and remained a kind of monument or Court of Appeal to which—at least as against all Arian teaching—reference could be made. But the term *ὁμοούσιος* had so bad a previous history, and could be so easily misunderstood to imply a doctrine at least as odious to the East at large as anything which it was meant to exclude, that constant attempts were made to find some other form of words. It was only when Arianism had taken courage from this wide-spread dislike of the Nicene formula and had laid bare its real character; only when the champions of the homo-ousian doctrine had convinced the uncertain and waverers that the term did not convey the Sabellian teaching which they feared still, though its foremost defenders had from the first disclaimed the Sabellian interpretation; only when every compromise had been tried and found wanting—it was only then that the term itself was finally accepted to express the doctrine which had all along been the implicit conviction of the great majority of churchmen. After prolonged discussion and dissension, after heated disputes and calm reflection, the word Homo-ousios triumphed over all competing terms of definition. Its most dangerous rival Homoi-ousios[1] was banished from orthodox usage with all the others. And so the *consensus fidelium*

[1] *Ὁμοιούσιος* or *ὅμοιος κατ' οὐσίαν* had served as a temporary bridge over the troubled waters, but it could give no permanent safety. Only when the *οὐσία* (Deity) was acknowledged as one and the same in Father and Son—only then was real stability secured.

at last pronounced the final verdict in favour of the term which Athanasius had all along declared was the only single term that safeguarded and expressed the continuous teaching of the Church. The final decision at Constantinople was a complete victory for the Nicene Creed and the doctrine of which Athanasius is commonly regarded as the chief literary and controversial representative.

This has been the settled historical tradition, universally accepted and expressed, at least in its main features, down to our own generation. But the nineteenth century, which has seen so many historical traditions unsettled and rejected or amended, has been obliged to reconsider the verdict of the ages on this matter too. The tradition has not indeed, so far as I am aware, been openly called in question: it has been quietly set aside or ignored. The undoubted fact of a certain change in terminology, by which *οὐσία* and *ὑπόστασις* (which to the framers of the Nicene Creed were synonymous) came to be discriminated, has been assumed to imply some corresponding change in the meaning of the word Homo-ousios itself. The Cappadocian fathers to whom the distinction between the two terms was mainly due are supposed to have attached to *ὁμοούσιος* a sense different from that which it conveyed to Athanasius and its champions at Nicaea. A 'new Nicene' party is assumed, and these 'young Nicenes'—the heirs of an Origenistic and a Homoi-ousian tradition—are supposed to have approached the question from so different a starting-point that though they accepted the Nicene term they read into it a meaning of their own.

To this new estimate of the doctrinal significance of the issues of the weary controversy which raged round the word wide currency has been given.

It is maintained that though Homo-ousios triumphed, yet it was accepted in the sense of Homoi-ousios; and much is made of opposition at the Council of Constantinople between what is called the 'old' (Nicene, Western, and Alexandrian) and the 'new' (Antiochene, Cappadocian, Asiatic) orthodoxy, though it is admitted that this opposition is only partly known to us.

Of old, it is argued, it had been the unity of the Godhead that had stood out plain and clear; the plurality had been a mystery. But after the Council of Alexandria in 362 it was permitted to make the unity the mystery—to start from the plurality and to reduce the unity to a matter of likeness; that is to say, to interpret Homo-ousios as Homoi-ousios, so changing the 'substantial' unity of being into mere likeness of being.

This is, in effect, to say that it was permitted to believe in three beings with natures like each other: *οὐσία* receiving a sense more nearly equivalent to 'nature' than to 'being'. And so instead of one Godhead, existing permanently—eternally—in three distinct forms or spheres of existence, there would be three forms of existence of like nature with one another, which together make up the Godhead. Such, it is said, was the Catholic faith as held by the leaders of the Church in the East and in the West (though more particularly in the East) at the end of the Arian controversy.

The first suggestion of this new reading of the history seems to have come from Dr Zahn in his admirable study of Marcellus, published in 1867[1]. Thenceforward it appears to have ousted the old tradition, being accepted incidentally by Professor Gwatkin[2], received with approval and emphasised by Dr Harnack in his *Dogmengeschichte*, 1886–1888, adopted without discussion by Dr Loofs[3], and as to the main conception—though not very clearly or consistently—by Dr Fisher in the latest *History of Christian Doctrine* that has been published in English[4].

Dr Harnack's authority has probably sufficed to convince all later writers[5]. His profound erudition and marvellous industry compel admiration and give unusual weight to any theory which he advocates. Every student of the history of the development of Christian doctrine gratefully recognises the value of the work he has done in amassing such stores of materials and presenting

[1] *Marcellus von Ancyra*, Gotha 1867, pp. 21, 87.

[2] *Studies of Arianism*, 1882, pp. 242, 262 (2nd ed. 1900, pp. 247 n. 1 and 270 n. 2).

[3] *Leitfaden zum Studium der Dogmengeschichte*³, p. 156 ff. (first edition pub. 1889).

[4] *History of Christian Doctrine* (International Theological Library), 1896, p. 143 ff.

[5] In England, at all events, for one who has read the monograph of Dr Zahn there are probably scores who have Dr Harnack's book in use.

them in clear and orderly form. At the same time he has so nobly expressed the ethical ideal by which all true historical investigation must be guided and controlled[1], that even his most startling utterances—his most revolutionary theories—come to us as the conclusions of one who, entirely disclaiming a point of view and having to the best of his ability weighed the evidence, presents the truth as it seems to him untrammelled by any traditional ties. Where is the student of history likely to find security, intellectual and moral, if not behind his aegis?

And so, for ten years past, as year by year it has been my duty to give such guidance as I could to students of the early history of Christian doctrines, I have drawn attention to the new view, as having the sanction of great names, though still demanding in my judgment to be further investigated, not less by the student whose only interest in the study is historical or antiquarian, than by all who believe in the general accuracy and truth of the results (the theories or doctrines) arrived at by the Church in the course of the various movements of the first four centuries of her life, and who accept in the main the historical theology and the traditional definitions of the Christian Faith.

It is the results of such further investigation on my own part that are offered here. Almost all the evidence has long been accessible to every student. Dr Harnack's *History of Doctrine* alone supplies us with nearly all the materials we can have, and with fruitful suggestions at every turn. We only have to use what is provided, bearing before us his motto that 'every historical study is an ethical task'.

But if such statements, on points of such importance, made in

[1] "In taking up a theological book we are in the habit of enquiring first of all "as to the 'standpoint' of the Author. In a historical work there is no room for "such enquiry. The question here is, whether the Author is in sympathy with "the subject about which he writes, whether he can distinguish original elements "from those that are derived, whether he has a thorough acquaintance with his "material, whether he is conscious of the limits of historical knowledge, and "whether he is truthful. These requirements constitute the categorical imperative "for the historian: but they can only be fulfilled by an unwearied self-discipline. "Hence every historical study is an ethical task. The historian ought to be "faithful in every sense of the word." *Author's Preface to the English Edition of the Dogmengeschichte.*

so positive a tone and with such authority, are to be examined at all, it is necessary to review the whole position. One cannot expect to find a single piece of fresh decisive evidence, though particular aspects of the case come home to oneself with fresh enlightening force[1]. But working quietly over the ground again and tracing the course of events, and trying to follow the intersecting streams of thought, I not only fail to find any certain positive evidence for the new assertions, but I find on the other hand much that tells against them.

First of all, however, let me state more fully and plainly the new interpretation of the history which is the justification for this new enquiry. It is given by Dr Harnack so clearly and forcibly that we cannot do better than quote his words. And no injustice will be done by isolating the statements from their context; for it is certain that they express in definite clear-cut outline the view which dominates his whole account of the course through which the controversy ran and of the significance of the final issue.

Dr Harnack's statements are as follows[2]:

First of all, writing of Theodosius, the Emperor, he says "This Council [of Constantinople 381] denotes a complete change "in the policy of Theodosius. His stay in the East had taught "him that it was necessary for him to recognise as orthodox all "who acknowledged the Nicene Creed however they might inter-"pret it....He had come to see that in the East he must rely

[1] For my own part I have come to realise much more clearly that ὁμοούσιος in the Creed is not as I, in common with many others, had supposed, a product of Greek philosophical thought, but rather of Latin theology. It is to the West we must look for the meaning it had to the framers of the Nicene Creed—and in the West in particular to Tertullian who so amazingly anticipated the later definitions of the Creeds. The meaning of οὐσία, moreover, and the permanent difference between it and φύσις (as in Latin between *substantia* and *natura*) has grown much more distinct. And the investigation of the history of the term *persona* and its theological usage has brought into clear relief the close relation subsisting between it and the corresponding Greek expressions which were used, and the difference between them all and our own term 'person'. Special attention may perhaps be invited to these three points.

[2] In the following passages the English translation in the *Theological Translation Library* (published by Williams and Norgate) is used, with occasional corrections or modifications.

"on the Eastern form of orthodoxy, the new orthodoxy....This "reversal of his policy is shewn most strikingly by the fact that "Meletius of Antioch was called upon to preside at the Council, "the very man who was specially suspected by the orthodox of "the West......The opposition between the old orthodox party "(orthodox in the Alexandrian and Western sense) and the new "orthodox party (composed of Antiochians, Cappadocians, and "Asiatics) was strongly expressed at the Council, though we are "only partially acquainted with it....Still union was finally "secured....The Nicene Creed thus gained an unqualified victory "so far as its actual terms were concerned, but understood accord-"ing to the interpretation of Meletius, the Cappadocians, and "Cyril of Jerusalem. *The community of substance in the sense of "likeness* (*or* equality) *of substance, not in that of unity of sub-"stance, was from this time the orthodox doctrine in the East.*" (*DG.*[3] vol. ii p. 262 ff., E. Tr. vol. iv p. 94 ff.)

Further, in regard to the Creed and its history, he says "This "much, however, is clear, that if this Creed had any connexion "at all with the Council of 381, the *neo-orthodox* character of the "latter is thereby brought out in a specially striking way; for the "*so-called creed of Constantinople can in fact be taken simply as a "formula of union between orthodox, Semi-Arians, and Pneumato-"machians.* The most contested phrase of the Nicene Creed *ἐκ "τῆς οὐσίας τοῦ πατρός* is wanting in it, and it presents the "doctrine of the Holy Spirit in a form which could have ap-"peared not wholly unacceptable even to the Pneumatomachians. "For this very reason it is certainly out of the question to "regard the Creed as the Creed of the Council of 381. It did "indeed assert the complete Homo-ousia of the Divine Persons. "But the legend manufactured in the Church by which this "Creed was attached to that Council performed a remarkable act "of justice; for in tracing back to this Council 'an enlarged "'Nicene Creed' without the *ἐκ τῆς οὐσίας τοῦ πατρός,* without "the Nicene anathemas, and without the avowal of the Homo-"ousia of the Spirit, and in attesting it as orthodox, it—without "wishing to do so—preserved the recollection of the fact that the "Eastern orthodoxy of 381 had really been a neo-orthodoxy, which "in its use of the word Ὁμοούσιος did not represent the dogmatic "conviction of Athanasius. In the *quid pro quo* involved in this "substitution of one Creed for another, we have a judicial sentence "which could not conceivably have been more discriminating; "but it involves still more than that—namely, the most cruel "satire. From the fact that in the Church the Creed of Con- "stantinople gradually came to be accepted as a perfect expression "of orthodoxy, and was spoken of as the Nicene Creed while the "latter was forgotten, it follows that the great difference which "existed between the old Faith and the Cappadocian neo-ortho- "doxy was no longer understood, and that under cover of the "Ὁμοούσιος a sort of Homoiousianism had in general been "reached, the view which has really been the orthodox one in all "Churches until this day. The father of the official doctrine "of the Trinity in the form in which the Churches have held "to it is not Athanasius, nor Basil of Caesarea, but Basil of "Ancyra." (*DG.*[3] vol. ii pp. 266, 267, E. Tr. vol. iv pp. 99, 100.)

And elsewhere "We may still further say it was not the "'Homoousios' which finally triumphed, but on the contrary the "Homoiousian doctrine, which fixed on the terms of agreement "with the Homoousios." (*DG.*[3] vol. ii p. 250, E. Tr. vol. iv p. 82.)

Such is Dr Harnack's statement of the case. He further says that special credit is due to Zahn for having been the first to draw attention to the facts, and he aims at justifying and supporting these assertions by notes on various points in detail[1]. (*DG.*[3] vol. ii p. 252, note 4, E. Tr. vol. iv p. 84.)

[1] In commenting on the lack of a precise and fixed terminology to express the 'subjects' in the one Godhead, through which (he says) Athanasius was betrayed at times, in contending against Sabellianism, into language contradictory to the Creed and to his own normal mode of speech (so as to deny that there was only one divine *οὐσία*, whereas he regularly maintained that the *οὐσία* of Father and Son was one and the same)—Zahn points to the fact that it was not to Athanasius that the development of any greater precision in the use of terms was due: he used to the last the words *οὐσία* and *ὑπόστασις* as equivalent terms. The fixing of the terminology was the work of the next generation—the younger Nicenes, the Cappadocian Fathers. But Zahn insists that it was not, however, a scientific perplexity which the young Nicenes overcame; but, on the contrary, that their so-called advance in the formal treatment of the matter really rested rather on a different conception of the relation which was to be expressed.

And so he says that after the synod of Seleucia, while the distinction between

For example, with regard to the absence of the phrase *ἐκ τῆς οὐσίας τοῦ πατρός* from the Creed which ultimately took the place of the Nicene Creed in the Church, he says "From the "writings of the Homoiousians and the Cappadocians we can "accordingly easily gather that the *ἐκ τῆς οὐσίας τοῦ πατρός* "presented a far greater difficulty to the half-friends of the "Nicene Creed than the *ὁμοούσιος*; for *ὁμοούσιος* not without "some show of fairness might be interpreted as *ὅμοιος κατ' οὐσίαν*, while on the contrary the *ἐκ τῆς οὐσίας* both in what "it said and in what it excluded—namely the will—seemed to "leave the door open to Sabellianism. It follows also from "Athanasius *de Synodis* that he considered *ἐκ τῆς οὐσίας* as of "supreme importance; for in a way that is very characteristic "of him he observes that *ὁμοούσιος* = *ὁμοιούσιος ἐκ τῆς οὐσίας*, "that is, whoever intentionally avows his belief in the *ὁμοούσιος* "without the *ἐκ τῆς οὐσίας* avows his belief in it as a Homoiousian. "The Christological formula in the Creed of Jerusalem, i.e. the "later Nicene-Constantinopolitan Creed, is thus almost homoi-"ousian, even although it retains the *ὁμοούσιος*." (*DG.*[3] vol. ii p. 266 n., E. Tr. vol. iv p. 99 n.)

And again the terms of the settlement are described in the following summary:—

"If up till now orthodox faith had meant the recognition of a "mysterious plurality in the substantial unity of the Godhead, it "was now made permissible to turn the unity into a mystery, i.e. "to reduce it to likeness (*or* equality) and to make the triad "(three-foldness) the starting-point; but this simply means that "*that Homoiousianism was recognised which resolved to accept the* "*word ὁμοούσιος.* And to this theology which changed the "substantial *unity* of substance expressed in the *ὁμοούσιος* into

οὐσία and *ὑπόστασις* became more established, the conception *οὐσία* was watered down more and more to mere mode of being (seinsweise), *ὁμοιότης* being mere similarity (aehnlichkeit) and 'homoousia' likeness (gleichartigkeit). And so "the Nicene "formula won the day in a different sense—in the East at least—from that in "which it had at first overcome Arianism." So too he points out that Epiphanius (*haer.* 73, 36) asserted that *ὁμοούσιος* did not mean what would be expressed by *ἀμαούσιος*: whereas, in fact, the only difference between the two words which the framers of the Nicene Creed would have recognised was that the one was Greek and the other was not. (Zahn *Marcellus* pp. 21—24.)

"a mere *likeness* (*or* equality) of substance, so that there was no "longer a threefold unity, but a trinity, the future belonged, in "the East, though not to the same extent in the West. The "theologians who had studied Origen regarded it with favour. "The Cappadocians started from the ὁμοιούσιος.... *They succeeded "in attaining terminological clearness...only because they modified "the original thought of Athanasius and developed the theology "which Basil of Ancyra had first propounded in his tractate.* "Οὐσία now got a meaning which was half-way between the "abstract 'substance' and the concrete 'individual substance'— "still it inclined very strongly in the direction of the former. "Ὑπόστασις got a meaning half-way between 'Person' and "'Attribute' (Accident, Modality), still the conception of Person "entered more largely into it.... The unity of the Godhead, as "the Cappadocians conceived of it, was not the same as the unity "which Athanasius had in his mind. Basil the Great was never "tired of emphasizing the new distinction implied in οὐσία and "ὑπόστασις." (*DG.*[3] vol. ii pp. 252—254, E. Tr. vol. iv pp. 84, 85.)

All this, and there is incidentally more to the same effect, amounts to saying that a doctrine which is hardly to be distinguished from polytheism, except in the limitation of the number of Gods to three, was ultimately accepted by the Church.

In order to form a judgment on these pronouncements we must examine first:

What ὁμοούσιος meant to those who proposed it at Nicaea (to the West—to Athanasius);

What ὁμοιούσιος meant to its champions and to Athanasius;

The position of Basil of Ancyra;

and then we can pass on to determine by closer scrutiny of the evidence available

(*a*) the sense in which Meletius and his party understood ὁμοούσιος;

(*b*) the sense in which the Cappadocians understood ὁμοούσιος, and the relations between them and Athanasius;

(c) the significance of the absence of ἐκ τῆς οὐσίας from the later Creed—(1) what this phrase meant to Athanasius; (2) how it happened, as a matter of fact, that it was not in the later Creed.

In the course of the enquiry it will be necessary to trace the history of the terms *substantia, οὐσία, ὑπόστασις*, and (incidentally) *natura* and *φύσις*, and *persona.*

What ὁμοούσιος meant to those who proposed it at Nicaea.

In considering the significance of the term ὁμοούσιος to the men who proposed it at Nicaea the dominant fact to bear in mind is that the suggestion came from the West and not from the East[1]. This fact has been noticed and generally acknowledged, but its full significance is less commonly recognised. Really, the West and Alexandria accepted ὁμοούσιος because they had long been used not only to the thought but also to the very term[2]; the East was not accustomed to the term, and—seeing the possibility of various objectionable interpretations of it—

[1] That Hosius—for many years previously the most influential bishop in the West, the intimate friend and trusted adviser in ecclesiastical matters of Constantine—was the real 'draftsman' of the Creed, seems certain. See P. B. Gams, *Die Kirchengeschichte von Spanien*, Bd ii Abth. 1 (pp. 137—309). In this connexion at all events it is a reversal of the facts to say that 'the Latins had received the rays of divine knowledge through the dark and doubtful medium of a translation', and that 'the poverty and stubbornness of their native tongue was not capable of affording just equivalents for the Greek terms'. (Gibbon *Decline and Fall of the Roman Empire* ch. xxi.)

[2] The very term, that is, in their own language—viz. *eiusdem* or *unius substantiae.* So it was that Hilary much later, thirty years after the Council, could write that long before he had ever heard the term ὁμοούσιος he had been familiar with the sense.—*De Syn.* § 91. (It is true he joins ὁμοιούσιος with it, but the whole drift of his argument is to shew that ὁμοιούσιος can only mean ὁμοούσιος—not *vice versa.* That is why a 'fidelis ac pia intelligentia' of ὁμοιούσιος is possible, because a thing cannot really be ὁμοιούσιον with another unless it is also ὁμοούσιον. See *De Syn.* § 76. Migne *Patr.* x p. 530. This is clearly an entirely different thing from taking ὁμοούσιος in the sense of ὁμοιούσιος.)

mistrusted its theological import[1]. All the weight of Western Conservatism was on its side; all the forces of Eastern Conservatism were united against it. Nor was it acquiesced in by the East—to anticipate for a moment the conclusion—till lapse of time had worn away its terrors, and repeated discussions had proved that none of the objectionable senses were intended, and its meaning had been fixed by a terminology which—leaving *οὐσία* to do duty for the sense which it bore to the champions of *ὁμοούσιος* at Nicaea and after—secured currency for another term (*ὑπόστασις*) to represent that possible sense of *οὐσία* which had given rise to the weightiest and most wide-spread opposition to *ὁμοούσιος* in the East.

All the evidence at the time, and all the subsequent history, which really centres in the suspicion and dread of Sabellianism, goes to shew that the main aim of the Nicenes was to insist on one *οὐσία* of the Godhead—to emphasise the one-ness and sole-ness of the Divine; and the equal participation in it of Father and Son was a necessary corollary for any one who accepted the doctrine of the divinity of the Son and regarded the Incarnation as a real revelation of God. That the *οὐσία* of the Son was the same as the *οὐσία* of the Father was the chief point, and obviously such a statement might easily be presented in a Sabellian light and might seem to endanger the distinction between Father and Son—while really being the only safeguard against the polytheistic interpretation of the doctrine of the divinity of both. So in the East it was only when terms were found, by which the necessary discrimination could be guaranteed, that the difficulty was overcome and union effected.

But in the West the terms were already in use and familiar to all theologians, more than a hundred years before the Council of Nicaea. The Latins were helped by the very poverty of their language. They simply had not got the terms to cause confusion. It is often stated that Tertullian fixed the terminology in which the Catholic doctrine of the Trinity was expressed. He did, no doubt; but he really had no choice. He found existing in the

[1] What all might know of the term was simply bad: that it had been employed in the past, but in such a sense that a Council condemning a mischievous heretic had ordered the word to be withdrawn from use.

language two words, and no more, which could be used—*substantia* and *persona*. He took them up and used them, and there were no other words which could attempt to oust them afterwards. So Latin theologians had the great advantage of a fixed and definite terminology at a time when in the East—for Greeks with their rich and varied phrases—there was no certainty at all[1].

It is therefore to the West that we must turn—to usage in the West before the Council of Nicaea—to see the meaning *ὁμοούσιος* had to Hosius and his allies[2]. It is the obvious Greek equivalent of the Latin [*unius* or] *eiusdem substantiae*, or of the less used adjectival forms *consubstantivus* and *consubstantialis*[3].

It is true the Greek term was first in the field[4]; but *not* in application to the doctrine of the Person of Christ and the Godhead.

This is the fact on which stress must be laid. In using the term in this—its later familiar—connexion, Latin theology has priority; and particularly its foremost representative Tertullian. Before his time the only Christians who had used it—so far as is known—were the Valentinians: and they had used it in other connexions. The sense which they attached to it is shewn by Irenaeus and by Tertullian himself.

[1] Similarly, *natura*, not much used at all in these connexions, and always as a characteristic of some *substantia*, never wavered in its meaning as did *φύσις* among Greek theologians.

[2] Zahn, p. 17, notes the lack of authentic, contemporary, evidence as to the sense intended by the original framers of the Creed—but the previous history of the term itself and of its Latin equivalent (which Zahn supplies) furnishes conclusive proof. So his statement that the word was first employed definitely in connexion with the Trinitarian doctrine of God in the correspondence between the two Dionysii must be corrected. Dionysius of Rome insisted on a term already perfectly familiar in the West. See *infra* p. 24. If he wrote in Greek, he was translating Latin thought.

[3] The old Latin versions of the Creed of Nicaea render the term by these phrases—(1) eiusdem substantiae qua Pater est, (2) consubstantialem Patri, (3) eiusdem cum Patre substantiae. See note in *Journal of Theological Studies*, Oct. 1900, by A. E. Burn.

[4] Harvey, *Iren.* vol. i p. 49, quotes Aristotle as using it to express the general sense of close relationship which exists between different members of the same cosmic order—one star is ὁμοούσιος with another star, and Porphyry as discussing the question εἴγε ὁμοούσιοι αἱ τῶν ζῴων ψυχαὶ ἡμετέραις.

The evidence of Irenaeus is as follows:

He says (Mass. I v 1—Harvey I i 9) that they held the spiritual part of the world (*τὸ πνευματικόν*) to be *ὁμοούσιον* with Achamoth who originates from and consists of the like *οὐσία*. And again (Mass. I v 4—H. I i 10) in describing the work of the creator of the world as depicted by them, he says "When he had created the world, he made also "the earthy man (*τὸν ἄνθρωπον τὸν χοϊκόν*)...and into him they declare "he breathed in the psychic man (*τὸν ψυχικόν*). He it is they say who "is the man made 'after the image and likeness'. The material man "(*τὸν ὑλικόν*) is 'after the image', nearly like but not of the same "*οὐσία* as God (*παραπλήσιον μὲν ἀλλ' οὐχ ὁμοούσιον τῷ θεῷ*). And the "psychic man is 'after the likeness', wherefore his *οὐσία* is said to be a "spirit of life, since it is from a spiritual effluence." And immediately after he says they taught that the offspring of the Mother herself (*or* their mother)—i.e. Achamoth,...being of the same *οὐσία* with the mother (*ὁμοούσιον ὑπάρχον τῇ μητρί*), is spiritual.

In all these instances the old Latin translation gives as equivalent to *ὁμοούσιος* *eiusdem substantiae*[1].

The same Latin is found in several other passages of which the Greek is not extant, and no doubt represents the same Greek word.

Thus (Mass. II xvii 3, 4, 7—H. II xxi, xxii) the question is discussed whether certain of the Aeons were *eiusdem substantiae* with those from which they proceeded, or had their *substantiam* derived *ex altera quadam substantia*[2]—the words recurring frequently in the discussion in these sections.

And (Mass. II xviii 5—H. II xxv), similarly, it is argued that the Aeon cannot be dissolved, nor suffer, since it is *eiusdem substantiae* as the Pleroma, and the Pleroma is entirely *ex Patre*.

And again (Mass. IV ix 1—H. IV iv 18), after shewing that the Law and the Gospel teaching are *unius et eiusdem substantiae, hoc est, ab uno et eodem Deo* (= Gk. *ἐκ μιᾶς καὶ τῆς αὐτῆς οὐσίας, τουτέστιν ἐξ ἑνὸς*

[1] The date of the Latin translation of Irenaeus is not known. It was certainly used by Augustine, and it may be as late as the fourth century—the great age of Latin translations. But it is perhaps almost contemporary with the original, and there are reasons for thinking that Tertullian, who wrote his treatise *adv. Valent.* after 199, had the Latin translation of Irenaeus before him (see Massuet's edition of Irenaeus p. ci f., Harvey vol. i p. clxiv, and J. R. Harris *Texts and Studies* vol. ii no. 1 p. 162 ff.). In any case, if it suggested the term *ὁμοούσιος* to Tertullian, the application which he made of it is his own, and he did not limit himself to one translation, v. *infra*.

[2] Cf. the phrase of the Nicene anathema *ἐξ ἑτέρας ὑποστάσεως ἢ οὐσίας*.

καὶ τοῦ αὐτοῦ θεοῦ), he argues with reference to Mt xii 6 that *plus* and *minus* are not said in respect of things which have not communion together, and are of contrary nature...but in respect of things which are *eiusdem substantiae* (in his quae eiusdem sunt substantiae et communicant secum, solum autem multitudine et magnitudine differunt: quemadmodum aqua ab aqua, et lumen a lumine, et gratia a gratia).

From these examples[1] it is clear that in all cases the term ὁμοούσιος is used of various forms of existence of one and the same *οὐσία*, all of which necessarily have all the characteristics which attach to that one and the same *οὐσία*, though they may have others also peculiar to themselves.

Tertullian's evidence is to the same effect.

In describing the conceptions of the Valentinians he uses the word *consubstantivus* (*adv. Valent.* 12, 18, cf. 37) to express a relation which connotes that the *substantia* of the subjects of comparison is one and the same, and that in virtue of it they are on the same level of rank and equality (*paria, coaequales*).

Writing against the 'materialist' Hermogenes (*adv. Hermog.* esp. 44) he uses another form of the word—*consubstantialis*—in a somewhat special sense. Hermogenes taught that the only hypothesis as to the creation of the world which could be maintained, in view of objections based on the existence of evil, was the hypothesis of the eternal existence of matter. There was thus always the *substantia* of God, and the *substantia* of matter—out of which God created the world. Further, as to the manner in which the work was carried out, he said creation was effected without any actual contact with matter, by the mere approach of God—by his mere appearance (as beauty makes its impression on the mind, or a magnet causes motion without actual contact). So matter was in part reduced to order and the ordered world (*mundus*, *κόσμος*) resulted, though part still remained outside the ordering influence (this being the source of evil). This subsidiary theory as to the mode of creation, Tertullian argues, is inconsistent with the hypothesis of the eternal existence of matter. For on this hypothesis there was no time when God had not appeared, had not been near, to matter. Both were eternal and God was always

[1] Add the passage M. II xiv 4, H. II xviii 4; and Heracleon *Comm. in Joann.* xiii 25, xx 18, of the relation between the Spiritual (pneumatic) and God, and between the Material (the hylic) and the Devil.

everywhere. Matter *ex hypothesi* was *consubstantialis* with him, and it was inconceivable that he could have been removed from it: indeed *qua* 'consubstantial' with him, it was as it were his own.

The sense of the word here seems to be 'equally a *substantia*' with him. Both alike were *substantiae*—two distinct existences; yet in virtue of its being also *substantia* as he himself was, matter might be said to be his own.

This is obviously a special and unique usage of the word, conditioned by the particular character of the conceptions in view: but it throws some side-light on the history of terms.

For the meaning of ὁμοούσιος in the Creed we must look to other writings of Tertullian, and particularly to the treatises against Praxeas and on the Soul.

It is in the treatise *on the Soul* that he marks most plainly the sense in which *substantia* was used by him, as indeed by all Western theologians after him. He sharply distinguishes *substantia* from *natura.* "Substance," he writes[1], "and the nature of "substance are different things. Substance is peculiar to each "particular thing, nature however can be shared with others "(*communis*). Take an example:—Stone and iron are substances: "the hardness of stone and of iron is the nature of the substance. "Hardness makes them partners (*communicat*), substance sets "them apart (*discordat*)......you mark the likeness of nature first, "when you observe the unlikeness of substance"—that is to say, you must first recognise that they are two as to substance before you can compare them as to nature. 'Substance' thus, it is clear, can never to Tertullian have the meaning 'nature'. *It* is not its nature. Its nature is not of course separated from it, but the thing itself cannot be its properties. The same nature *may* be characteristic of several particular substances; the substances might be different, though their natures were the same. But if the substance is one, the nature also will be one. It must have its proper nature. Accordingly, if the *substantia* is spoken of, its *natura* is necessarily understood and need not be asserted; but it is not enough to speak of *natura* only. You might assert 'of one nature' while denying 'of one substance'.

[1] *de Anima* 32. In like manner e.g. *adv. Prax.* 26 he distinguishes between *substantia* and the *accidentia* or *proprietates uniuscuiusque substantiae.*

The recognition of this clear distinction is the chief clue to the maze of subsequent theological controversy—a clue however which was not possessed by many of those who had to thread its winding paths.

Thus it is that Tertullian does not speak of 'nature' in connexion with the doctrine of the Godhead which he expounds, but is able equally well to describe the being of God as 'one substance' and the person of Christ as combining in himself 'two substances'. God—deity—is one substance; Man—humanity—is another. There is no contradiction or confusion of thought in speaking, as regards the being of God, of one substance and three persons, and as regards the constitution of the person of Christ of two substances and one person—he being at once God and man.

In this way the unity of the Godhead is strongly marked—it is one and the same *substantia* of Godhead which all three share alike. This is "the mystery of the providential order which "arranges the unity in a trinity, setting in their order three— "Father, Son, and Holy Spirit; three however not in condition "but in relation, and not in substance but in form, and not in "power but in aspect: nay, rather, of one substance and of one "condition and of one power, inasmuch as it is one God from whom "these relations and forms and aspects are reckoned in the name "of Father and of Son and of Holy Spirit" (*adv. Prax.* 2)[1]. And again he speaks of 'one substance in three who together form the whole (*in tribus cohaerentibus*)' (*ib.* 12). Everything is included in the designation *unius substantiae*:—the additional phrases 'of one condition' (*status*—i.e. the whole legal position and qualities) and 'of one power' are only amplifications. It is *una substantia* which exists in three relations[1] or forms or aspects or persons—though Tertullian does not use the last word freely. He only has the definite expression when it cannot be

[1] Cf. Bull's statement of the case (*Def. Fid. N.* II vii 6) 'the order whereby the Father exists of himself, the Son goes forth immediately from the Father, and the Holy Spirit proceeds from the Father through the Son; so that the Father is rightly designated the first, the Son the second, and the Holy Spirit the third Person of the Godhead.' Between *species* and *forma* there is no perceptible difference—at least Cicero, *Top.* 7 (cited by Forcellini), says the same thing is signified by *species* as by *forma*.

omitted[1]. He prefers to speak of 'three' without further designation than the names they bear.

"The connexion of the Father in the Son and of the Son in "the Paraclete produces three coherent to each other. And "these three are one, but not one in number (*unum non unus*); as "it was said, I and the Father are One (*unum*), in regard to unity "of substance, not in regard to singularity of number[2]."

The employment of the terms which are used, and the avoidance of the use of other terms, shews that anxious as Tertullian was to overthrow the conceptions of Monarchians he was no less determined to maintain the oneness of the Godhead as the starting point. Concerned to realise the distinctions represented by the three Names in the Godhead, he was as precise as possible as to the identity of the divine being which exists in those three relations, forms, or aspects. In these expressions he is feeling after some clearer terminology to describe at once the unity of the divine existence and the diversity of relations within the unity, alike in its inward and in its manifested life. By *formae* and *species* (forms and aspects) he means exactly what the Cappadocians meant by 'modes of existence', τρόποι ὑπάρξεως. By *gradus* (degree or relation) he has obviously no intention of indicating any kind of inequality as to the one divine *substantia—status—potestas*: he simply means to express the conception of ordered relation between the three[3].

That this is so may be seen from careful consideration of the language of the treatise against Praxeas, in spite of occasional

[1] e.g. *adv. Prax.* 26 when supporting the doctrine of the Trinity from the baptismal commission he writes 'nam nec semel, sed ter, ad singula nomina in personas singulas tinguimur.' In like manner Augustine while feeling compelled to speak of three 'persons', apologised for the term and threw the responsibility for it on to the poverty of the language. They must say *personae*, because *there are three* —'tamen cum quaeritur *quid* tres, magna prorsus inopia humanum laborat eloquium. Dictum est tamen tres personae, non ut illud diceretur, sed ne taceretur.' *de Trin.* v 10, cf. vii 7—10. (On the other hand Tertullian has no scruple about using the term of Jesus Christ, both man and God—combining in himself the two *substantiae*, but being one Person, having the *status* of each substance: 'videmus duplicem statum, non confusum, sed coniunctum in una persona, deum et hominem Jesum', *adv. Prax.* 27.)

[2] *adv. Prax.* 25. [See additional Note on *Persona* p. 70 *infra*.]

[3] See note 1, p. 17.

expressions which, if isolated, might support a different view. 'The Son I derive,' he says, 'from no other source but from the substance of the Father[1]'—where the 'substance of the Father' is only (as it was later to Athanasius) a safeguard against misunderstanding to which the simple phrase 'the Father' might be liable: elsewhere he can use the single word—'We say that the Son is produced (projected) from the Father, but not separated from him[2].' So he who is emitted from the substance of the Father must of course be of that substance[3], and there is no separation between the two. The Word is 'always in the Father ...and always with God...and never separated from the Father or different from the Father.' He speaks, it is true, of the Father as being 'the whole substance', while the Son is 'a derivation from, and portion of, the whole' and so 'made less' than the Father[4]—but only for the purpose of marking the distinction as real, and involving no diversity between them and no division of the one substance. The relation between them may be illustrated by human analogies. The root produces (emits) the shrub, the spring the stream, the sun the ray. The former is in each case as it were the parent, and the latter the offspring. They are two things, but they are inseparably connected: the being of both is one and the same[5]. That which proceeds, moreover, is second to that from which it proceeds, and when you say 'second' you say that there are two. It is in order to mark clearly the distinct personality of the Son that he calls him 'second'. There is no suggestion or thought of subordination in any other sense than in regard to origin, and even that is merged in the unity of substance. In the case under consideration there is a third. 'The Spirit is third from God and the Son, just as the fruit which comes from the shrub is third from the root, and the river which flows from the stream is third from the spring, and the peak of the ray third from the sun[6].' There is

[1] *adv. Prax.* 4 'filium non aliunde deduco sed de substantia patris.'

[2] *ib.* 8. [3] *ib.* 7. [4] *ib.* 9. Cf. note 1, p. 20.

[5] So § 13 with reference to the simile of the sun and its ray—not making two suns, yet to be accounted 'tam duas res et *duas species unius et indivisae substantiae*...quam deum et sermonem eius, quam patrem et filium.'

[6] *adv. Prax.* 8.

moreover a sense in which the Father is one, and the Son other, and the Spirit yet other; as he who generates is other than he who is generated; and he who sends than he who is sent[1]. Yet there is no division of the one substance, though there are three in it, each of whom is a substantive existence, of the substance of the Godhead[2]. That is to say—there is the one substance—God or Godhead; and in it, making it up, are three forms or modes of existence, each real (a *substantiva res*)[1]. So it is 'a Trinity of one divinity[3].'

Seizing the Monarchian watchword he turns it against themselves, and insists that no rule or government is so much the rule of a single person, so much a 'monarchy,' that it cannot be administered through others appointed to fulfil their functions by the monarch. The monarchy is not divided and does not cease to be a monarchy, if the monarch's son is associated with him in the rule. The kingdom is still the king's: its unity is not impaired[4].

That God the Father was never really alone—since there was always with him the Logos as his reason and word—is shewn by the analogy of the operation of human thought and consciousness[5], and by the very name of Father—which implies the existence of the Son (he had a Son but was not himself his Son)—as well as by numerous passages of the Scriptures. But between him and the Son there was no division, though they were two (and though it would be better to have two divided Gods than the one 'change-coat' God the Monarchians preached).

The treatise against Praxeas is more technical in phraseology and definitely theological in purpose than the *Apology*; but in the latter—intended for more general reading—the same doctrine is expressed in somewhat different language.

The Son is *de substantia Patris* (ἐκ τῆς οὐσίας τοῦ πατρός) and therefore also *unius substantiae* (ὁμοούσιος) with the Father[6].

[1] *adv. Prax.* 9.

[2] *ib.* 26. This is Tertullian's conception, though he can also speak of the Father as 'tota substantia', and it became the custom—in order to safeguard the unity of the Godhead—to conceive of the divine being as primarily subsistent in the Father. See *infra* pp. 29, 30.

[3] *de Pudicitia* 21. [4] *adv. Prax.* 3. [5] *ib.* 5.

[6] This is the effect of the terms used. Spirit is a *substantia*, and God is Spirit. The Logos is *ex deo prolatus* and is called God *ex unitate substantiae*. The *sub-*

What Tertullian meant by *substantia* is shewn in the passages cited. The philosophical term is used in its proper sense as the natural Latin equivalent of *ὑπόστασις* or *οὐσία* (see the special note on the words). But Tertullian was more a jurist than a philosopher, and light is thrown on his usage by reference to the legal significance of the terms he employs[1]. Substance (*substantia*) meant 'property'—the sense in which we still use the word when we speak of a 'man of substance'—a man's possessions, estate, fortune: the owner's rights in which were carefully protected by Roman law from invasion or infringement. Person (*persona*) meant a being with legal rights, a 'party' in an action at law, an individual whose being as such was recognised by law as one of the facts of which it took cognisance—a real existence (*res*) within its own limitations. Such a person's position or circumstances would be his status or condition (*status, condicio*); perhaps even his nature (*natura* or *proprietas*) when looked at from a more inward point of view; and obviously a number of persons might occupy the same status or be in the same condition or have the same nature. So too there might be various kinds of 'substance,' each marked by special characteristics or 'properties' (in the sense of that which is proper or peculiar to each) or 'nature' (*proprietates, natura*).

So, if these human analogies be applied to the interpretation of the Christian revelation, one 'substance' is divinity—all that belongs to and goes to make up the divine existence. This is, as it were, one piece of property. But, following the human analogy, there is nothing to hinder its being held in joint ownership by three individuals with the same rights in it on equal terms—each being owner to the full, but the three always acting as one. And so the description of the divine existence would be *una substantia, tres personae, in uno statu*.

stantia of both is one and the same (*nec separatur substantia, sed extenditur*). They are two *modulo, non numero; gradu, non statu* (*Apol.* 21).

[1] Harnack directs attention to the point, *DG.*[3] ii p. 285 ff., E. Tr. iv pp. 122, 123; but he seems to attach undue importance to a usage which does not appear in any special manner dominant in Tertullian's treatment of the matter. It is sufficient to note the usage as offering a suggestive illustration rather than as determining the conception.

But there is also another 'substance'—all that belongs to and goes to make up human existence, all that is owned by men *qua* men. This is another piece of property, and still from the point of view of Roman law there is nothing to hinder one and the same person from holding at the same time two quite different pieces of property. So the two 'substances,' divinity and humanity, might be owned and all the rights and privileges attaching to each exercised and enjoyed, at one and the same time, by one and the same person, Jesus Christ.

These illustrations from the legal significance of the terms are no doubt suggestive, but that it is going too far to describe Tertullian's conceptions as in any way controlled by juristic usage is proved by the argument of the passages already quoted—particularly the special discussion in the *de Anima*—and by the treatment of the relation between the spirit and the flesh in the constitution of the person of Jesus Christ in the treatise against Praxeas (§ 27). It was not, he maintains, that the spirit was transformed (*transfiguratus*) when he became flesh, but that 'he put on' flesh. God, as being eternal, is unchangeable and incapable of being transformed. To have been transformed would have been to have ceased to be God. But the Logos never ceased to be what he was to begin with. If the Logos had really become flesh by any process of transformation and change of 'substance,' then Jesus would have been a new 'substance' formed out of the two 'substances' flesh and spirit—a kind of mixture, a *tertium quid.* But there was no kind of mixture[1]: each 'substance' remained distinct in its own characteristics—the Word was never anything but God, the flesh was never anything but man. He who was Son of God as regards the spirit, was man and son of man. "We see," he says, "the double *status* (the two not confused "but conjoined in one person), God and man Jesus [*or* God and

[1] This passage must correct the careless expression 'homo Deo mixtus' of the *Apology* (c. 21). He expressly repudiates the conception of any kind of mixture, using the illustration of *electrum*, a compound of gold and silver, neither the one thing nor the other, to shew what Jesus Christ was *not.* Cf. also *de Carne Christi*, esp. § 18, where he insists on the distinct origin of the spirit and the flesh, and discusses the interpretation of John iii 6 as spoken by Christ of himself, shewing that each remains what it was.

"the man Jesus]." This is Christ. "And the peculiar properties "of each 'substance' are preserved intact, so that in him the "spirit conducted its own affairs—that is, the deeds of power and "works and signs—and the flesh underwent its sufferings, hunger-"ing in the instance of the Devil (sc. the temptation), thirsting in "the instance of the Samaritan woman, weeping for Lazarus, "sorrowful unto death; and finally it died." It is clear, he insists, that both 'substances' exercised their functions each by itself. *Qua* flesh and man and Son of man he died; *qua* Spirit and Word and Son of God he was immortal[1].

It is thus abundantly clear that familiar as Tertullian was with the legal usage of the terms in question, his conception of *substantia* will not be brought under any such limited use. It is that which underlies things and makes them what they are—the reality of the things themselves—to which all the particular properties of the things adhere. [See additional Note on *Substantia* p. 65 *infra.*]

After Tertullian there was no great theological Latin writer till the Arian controversy was nearing its close. By his accurate definition and terse and pregnant description he fixed the value of terms and effectively moulded the Latin language to the service of ecclesiastical needs, and fashioned the formulas of Western orthodoxy. The *Da magistrum* of Cyprian[2] represents in effect the attitude of the leaders of Western theology towards him. It is

[1] So "It is not in respect of the divine substance, but in respect of the human substance, that we say he died," *adv. Prax.* 29, where he has the interesting argument against the conception that the Father 'suffered with' the Son, based mainly on the ground that in the divine substance, which was all that the Father and the Son had in common, the Son himself did not suffer.

Cf. also *de Carne Christi*, § 5, on the different parts played by the two substances. He speaks of the *utriusque substantiae census* (? the registering of each substance—his being classed under each substance) as proving him man and God, and then goes on to refer to the characteristics of each 'substance' as its *condicio* and *natura*.

[2] Jerome *de vir. ill.* 53 relates at second-hand the reminiscence of Cyprian's *notarius* that he never passed a day without reading Tertullian. (For a similar appreciation of his merits at a later time see Vincent *Commonit.* 18 (24) 47.) On the other hand Eusebius seems to have been the only Greek writer who knew him, and that probably only through a Greek translation of the *Apology* (*H. E.* ii 2. 4).

his teaching that lies at the back of subsequent Latin thought, his terms that became traditional: his doctrine that banished Arianism as it had dealt the death-blow to pure Monarchian caution: his very words in which at the end of the Christological controversies of the fifth century the teaching of the Church was summed up.

That the theology of Tertullian was accepted at Rome is shewn by the next important Latin writing, the *De Trinitate* of Novatian, which was styled by Jerome[1] an 'epitome of Tertullian's work' and is described by Dr Harnack as creating for the West a dogmatic *vade mecum.* It is true there are some phrases which might be taken to imply some vagueness of conception as to the real eternity of the Son, but they are balanced by others in which the sonship is shewn to be contemporaneous with the fatherhood[2]. And inasmuch as exposition, rather than refutation of error, is the main purpose of the treatise, there is not in it the same precision of language as Tertullian's pointed epigrams afford. But the two *substantiae* in Christ are asserted in the same sense (*utraque substantia...Deus et homo*, § 13), and the use of the phrase *substantiae communio* (§ 31) to express the relation between Father and Son shews that the doctrine of the *una et eadem substantia* was the basis of the entire exposition[3]. [This being clearly asserted, it is of course open to him to speak of the union as concord and moral harmony, as when in expounding the *personarum distinctio* he says Christ is a 'secunda persona post Patrem' (§ 26) and that he shewed the 'proprietas personae suae' when he said 'I and the Father' and used the plural *sumus*, while by the *unum* he shewed the 'societatis concordia' (§ 27).]

It is accordingly from Rome that the term *unius substantiae*

[1] The authority of Jerome, *de vir. ill.* c. 70, who names the treatise as Novatian's (while he notes that many 'who did not know' thought it was Cyprian's or Tertullian's), may be accepted in spite of more modern doubts. Cf. Harnack, *Gesch. der altchristl. Litt.* i 652—656.

[2] Such phrases as 'hic ergo, quando pater voluit, processit ex patre', 'necesse est prior sit, qua pater sit', but also 'semper enim in patre, ne pater non semper sit pater.' Also the idea that the kingdom of the Son would not be everlasting (as Origen and Marcellus)—but this speculative thought is not necessarily inconsistent with an eternal distinction within the Divine Being.

[3] So Harnack notes (*DG.* i p. 543 n) that in the fourth century all the Novatians were orthodox-Nicene.

(ὁμοούσιος) is pressed on Dionysius of Alexandria for acceptance. It is Rome that supports the protest against the doctrine of τρεῖς ὑποστάσεις in the Godhead—a doctrine that was of course expressed in Latin by the synonym *tres substantiae* (as to most Greeks at the time it must have been equivalent to τρεῖς οὐσίαι) and seemed utterly to overthrow the unity of the *substantia* of the Godhead. Whether Dionysius of Rome actually wrote in Greek or in Latin to his namesake, there can be little question that he thought in Latin and had been taught the faith and was accustomed in turn to teach it at Rome in Latin and not in Greek[1]. It is the traditional Latin doctrine in the traditional terms that he quietly lays down for the instruction of his Alexandrian brother. That the latter, though accepting the term ὁμοούσιος, as consonant with what he found in the Scriptures and really believed and taught, did not grasp its full significance may be inferred from his use of the words ὁμοφυής and ὁμογενής as near equivalents in the explanations which he gives of the analogies he had used to shew the relation between the Father and the Son (Ath. *de Sent. Dionys.* § 18). He says he recognised that, as being Son and Logos, he could not be alien from the being (essence) of the Father (ξένος τῆς οὐσίας τοῦ π. § 20): but in his anxiety to resist all forms of Sabellian teaching he would, if left to himself, it seems, prefer some mode of expression which laid less emphasis on the *identity* of οὐσία. Athanasius no doubt puts the best complexion on the case, and cites the phrases from his *Refutation and Defence* which tell most strongly in favour of the Nicene side: but they shew Dionysius insisting still on τρεῖς ὑποστάσεις (at a time when ὑπόστασις could scarcely be distinguished from οὐσία[2]) and only repudiating the idea that the three names were separable or divisible or could be parted or sundered one from another (§ 17). Stress must be laid

[1] Even if the unproved theory of the long continuance of the use of the Greek language in the Church of Rome be accepted, there cannot be much doubt that by the middle of the third century Latin was firmly established—even though a scholar might write in Greek and both languages were widely understood. The preservation of writings of earlier members of the Church of Rome in Greek only is perhaps partly accidental.

[2] Cf. the reference to him in Basil *Ep.* ix as not content with declaring a difference of hypostases but going so far as to assert a difference of substance.

on this evidence because its precise significance is not always appreciated. It is quite clear that Dionysius heartily held the unity—the identity—of *nature* between Father and Son. His hesitation to accept *unius substantiae* or ὁμοούσιος shews that he knew that something more than 'identity of nature' was meant by the term: nothing less indeed than identity of being—*una substantia, μία οὐσία*[1]. He cannot resist the arguments (which we can easily infer) which were used to convince him that this is the true expression; but for himself he continues to think more naturally on the lines on which he had been before. That is to say, he realises one nature more readily than one *οὐσία* of Godhead.

Rome and the West taught by Tertullian was not content with one nature and insisted on one substance or essence or being. The memory of this no doubt remained at Alexandria during the following fifty years and prepared the way for the acceptance of the Western doctrine at Nicaea.

The possible use of the term ὁμοούσιος by Origen before this time and its condemnation in the farther East at Antioch in 269, a little later than the discussion between the Dionysii, contribute nothing towards the purpose before us.

That Origen really held the doctrine for which ὁμοούσιος stands seems certain[2]. The very *raison d'être* of the Logos he represents as

[1] So Zahn, *l.c.* pp. 14, 15, rightly maintains that ὁμοούσιος was employed to safeguard the one-ness of the Godhead against undue emphasis of the personal distinctions (rather than to counteract undue subordination of the Son to the Father), and that the special feature of Arian teaching which wounded the theological consciousness of others was not the dishonouring of the Logos or the denial of his co-eternity with the Father, but the polytheistic tendency which was at once perceived in it. (It is noteworthy that it was a discourse of Bp Alexander about the Monad in the Triad which gave occasion to Arius to set out his conceptions, Socr. *H. E.* i 5 and Euseb. *Vit. Const.* ii 69.) The reply of Dionysius shews that in his view the question at issue was not the co-ordination or subordination, nor the likeness or difference, but the union or separation, of the Son and the Father; and that he recognised a *συνάφεια* and *κοινωνία* of the Trinity which made the use of the singular number legitimate.

[2] Bigg, *Christian Platonists*, p. 179, insists that it could not be his definite opinion, because (1) *οὐσία* still means at times person or hypostasis, (2) it was not clear that God had *οὐσία* at all—he was rather above all *οὐσία—ἐπέκεινα τῆς οὐσίας*, cf. *Contra Celsum* vi 64, (3) the word belongs to the vocabulary of science and not

the purpose of revealing God; and for this reason he has a personal subsistence side by side with the Father and must be (if he is to reveal him truly), as regards his being, of one essence with God. He must be in his own being God, and not only as sharing in the being of God. (See *de Princip.* i 2 6, i 2 2.) The evidence of Pamphilus (in the Latin translation of Rufinus) that he used the very word may perhaps not be regarded as conclusive [Apology for Origen c. 5 p. 33 quoting from Origen's commentary on the Epistle to the Hebrews 'And these simili- 'tudes...shew most clearly that the Son has communion of substance '(essence) with the Father; for an effluence is seen to be *homoousios*, 'that is of one substance (essence), with the body of which it is an 'effluence or vapour']. But if he did, it is probable he was using *οὐσία* rather in its secondary sense of nature than in the stricter concrete sense of being or existence—*substantia.* (Cf. what he says *de Princip.* i 2 5 'the only one who is by nature a Son, and is therefore termed the 'Only-begotten'; *ib.* i 2 10 'in all respects incapable of change or altera- 'tion, and every good quality in him being essential and such as cannot 'be changed or converted'; *ib.* i 2 12 'there is no dissimilarity whatever 'between the Son and the Father'—and the similitudes *ib.* ii 6 6 and i 2 8.)

What happened at Antioch we do not know. The Council which condemned Paul condemned also the use of the word ὁμοούσιος; but whether it was that Paul had used the word himself, or that he was able to produce ingenious arguments against it, must remain uncertain. The accounts of Athanasius, Hilary, and Basil are at variance.

Athanasius (*de Syn.* 45), having said that he has not himself seen the bishops' letter, accepts the statement of the Semi-Arians that it was rejected because it was taken in a material sense and because Paul used the sophistical reasoning that 'if Christ did not become God after 'starting as man, he is ὁμοούσιος with the Father, and there must 'therefore be three οὐσίαι, one principal and the two derived from it'— so that to guard against such argument they said Christ was not ὁμο- ούσιος, the Son not being related to the Father as Paul imagined.

Hilary (*de Syn.* 81, 86) implies that the word was used by Paul to express the idea that Father and Son were of one single and solitary being: but this would be more like the teaching of Sabellius than of Paul. [It is possible that objection was taken to Paul's reasoning that the Logos was one person with God as the reason is one with man, on

of Scripture, and οὐσία is precisely that about a thing of which we are wholly ignorant.

the ground that the doctrine of the Church required one God but more than one *πρόσωπον*, and that to meet this objection he declared that he recognised such *πρόσωπα*—God and Christ standing over against each other as *ὁμοούσιοι*—meaning equally existent or alike personal (each an *οὐσία*—*οὐσία* being taken in the sense of particular individual being, *τόδε τι*). But this, in the opinion of his opponents, would be hopelessly to confuse the issues, and so the word would be rejected. It is of course quite clear that if *οὐσία* were taken in the sense of *substantia* or essence Paul could not have accepted the term.]

Basil (*Ep.* 52), on the other hand, so far agrees with the account that Athanasius gives as to represent Paul as the objector, with an argument against the word which was certainly familiar in later times: viz. that if Christ was not made God out of (after being) man, but was *ὁμοούσιος*, then there must have been some common *οὐσία* of which they both partook, distinct from and prior to the divine persons themselves, and that out of it two beings—the Father and the Son—were produced as two coins are struck out of the same metal.

The term may therefore have been withdrawn (as Bull *D.F.N.* II i 13 and Newman *Arians* ch. i suggest) as being likely to perplex weak minds. In any case, as Athanasius, caring as always little for the words and much for the sense, insists, it was capable of being understood in different ways, and it was rejected in one sense by those who condemned the Samosatene and championed in another sense by those who resisted the Arian heresy. "It is unbecoming to "make the one conflict with the others; for all are fathers; nor is it "pious to determine that the ones spoke well and the others ill; for "all of them fell asleep in Christ (*de Syn.* 43)." "Yes, surely, each "Council has a sufficient reason for its own language."

From the time of the Dionysii to the outbreak of the Arian controversy no further question seems to have arisen.

The previous history of the word, accordingly, makes clear its meaning in the Creed—in spite of the lack of authentic contemporary evidence, and even if we were obliged to regard the testimony of Eusebius of Caesarea as 'a mixture of theological incapacity and disingenuousness' (as Zahn p. 18). It is the meaning revealed by Basil of Ancyra at a later time, when he gives *ταὐτούσιος* as its equivalent (Epiph. *adv. Haer.* 73, 11) and shews the fear that the personal distinction might seem to be endangered by such a *ταὐτότης* of *οὐσία*. There can be no doubt that *οὐσία* is here *substantia* and not 'nature'. And it is the same explanation that is given by Athanasius (whose share in the proceedings at Nicaea was probably unimportant), when he first handles the question twenty-five years later in the *de Decretis* "at a time when the incessantly "reiterated reproach of Sabellianism began to be troublesome to "the Nicenes" (Zahn[1]). The term ὁμοούσιον, as he explains it, stands for the unity of God; not the mere likeness of Father and Son:—they are not merely like, but the same in likeness (§ 20): and he argues that 'like' ὅμοιος was not enough, because individuals belonging to a *genus*, as human father and son, in spite of full likeness could be separated and far apart from one another; whereas the Logos is inseparable from the Being of the Father and one with him (§ 20). And again, he insists that the Son cannot be thought of as an accident or attribute of the conception of God, as though God were a compound—God who is the Father being the οὐσία and the Son being a συμβεβηκός or ποιότης; but that he belongs essentially to the being of the Father (§§ 17, 22, 27)[2]. It is from this essential unity that there follows equally the unchangeableness of nature without which the Son could not remain identical with himself[3], and the sameness of being without which he could not be thought of as one with the Father (the ταὐτότης πρὸς τὸν ἑαυτοῦ πατέρα of *de Decr.* 23, 24 etc.). So Athanasius can speak of a μονὰς τῆς θεότητος and a ἑνότης τῆς οὐσίας (*Or. c. Ar.* iv 1). The divine οὐσία (or ὑπόστασις) or θεότης is—as Zahn, pp. 20, 21, describes it —that which goes through the three subjects and underlies the "accidental" relations (in respect of which Father, Son and Spirit are different). Μία θεότης and εἷς θεός are synonymous conceptions, and the οὐσία of God is God himself (see esp. *de Decr.* 22), numerically one. To this οὐσία must be referred all predicates and

[1] Zahn cites nearly all the passages which are referred to in this section. See also note on "like the Father", *infra* p. 31.

[2] Cf. *Or. c. Ar.* iv 2, and *ad Afros* 8, where arguing against the idea that the relation of the Son to the Father is merely ethical, he says that if it is from virtue, will, and moral progress...that they hold the Son to be like the Father, these things fall under the category of quality—and so they would be calling God compound of quality and essence. "But who will tolerate you when you say this?" Cf. also *de Decr.* 15, 22.

[3] Cf. *Or. c. Ar.* i 22, and *infra* p. 47 note 2.

attributes—" we believe one Godhead and that the nature of this " Godhead is one (Ath. *ad Antiochenos* §§ 5, 6)[1]"—and all (personal) distinctions in the Godhead. It is the underlying Being (Essence) 'which must be represented as a concrete if one is to be able to speak of God as one' (Zahn). The unity of Being recognised by the Church and expressed in the Nicene Creed could not be realised unless the *οὐσία,* the subject of the predicates Father, Son, Holy Spirit, was conceived as one and the same, continuous and unbroken through generation or procession (cf. *de Syn.* 50). It is just because the *οὐσία* is the same that all the same divine predicates are applied in the Scriptures to the Son as to the Father, except the one predicate Father (*id.* 48, 49). The whole divine being dwells alike in Father, Son, and Holy Spirit.

The Father is only one of the subjects of the Triad, and cannot be thought of as existing apart from the other Two. But He is commonly represented in a special relation as either the summit which keeps together the whole divine being (Dionysius), or the beginning, the source or foundation of it (Ath. *Or. c. Ar.* iii 15, iv 1)—that which made the unity in God possible. From the standpoint of this conception the Divine Being is primarily subsistent in the Father; and perhaps objections to the term ὁμοούσιος led its champions to lay undue emphasis on the priority of the Father.

The testimony of passages such as these leaves us in no doubt as to the meaning of *οὐσία* and *ὁμοούσιος* to Athanasius. Moreover, the charge of Sabellianism, which was always brought against the chief supporters of the Homo-ousian doctrine, also shews conclusively that they were believed to use the terms in this sense.

What ὁμοιούσιος meant to its champions and to Athanasius.

It was precisely to oppose this apparently Sabellian doctrine that *ὁμοιούσιος* was invented as a substitute. Its supporters believed the *nature* of the three 'persons' to be the same, divine; but the *οὐσία* was only like, and so there was no fear of the notion of one personal God appearing in different forms at different times:—there were three beings, whose underlying essences were

[1] The distinction is clearly drawn between the *οὐσία—θεότης*—and its *φύσις.*

'like', but the essence was of higher quality or superior quantity in one than in another[1].

That is to say, against a doctrine which, though it was Trinitarian, insisted on the oneness of the Divine Being which was in the Three, there was set up a doctrine which however disguised was essentially polytheistic.

And this is the doctrine which, tracing the genealogical descent

[1] That this was the significance of ὁμοιούσιος both to its champions and to its opponents will not be disputed. A few points only need be noted.

To say that the Son is 'like' the Father is not at first sight open to objection. The expression had been widely current without protest. Athanasius in his earlier treatises against the Arians was content to speak of the Son as being like the Father (see e.g. the *Depositio Arii*, c. 323, and the *Expositio Fidei*, ? 328 A.D., Hahn[3] p. 264), and in argument with Arians he does not disallow the term even later (*Or. c. Ar.* ii 34, 356—360, cf. *ad Afros* 7, c. 369). But at this later time he used it himself only with qualification (e.g. *Or. c. Ar.* ii 22, κατὰ πάντα, and i 40, iii 20, but alone ii 17).

So Cyril of Jerusalem in his Catechetical Lectures (348—350), while insisting on the necessity of Scriptural language and contradicting the doctrines of Arius (without mentioning his name), protests against terms of human contrivance (*Cat.* v 12) and uses 'like the Father' *either* 'according to the Scriptures' *or* 'in all things'.

But as early as *de Decr.* 20 (c. 351—355), Athanasius had written that by saying the Son was "one in οὐσία" with the Father the Council meant "that the "Son was from the Father, and not merely like but the same in likeness...", his likeness being different from such as is ascribed to us: and he proceeded to shew (§ 23) that mere likeness implies something of difference. "Nor is he like only outwardly, "lest he seem in some respect or wholly to be other in οὐσία, as brass shines like "gold or silver or tin. For these are foreign and of other kind and separated off "from each other in nature and quality, nor does brass belong to gold...but though "they are considered like, they differ in essence." And later, *de Syn.* 53 (c. 359—361), he argued altogether against the use of the term 'like' in connexion with οὐσία on the ground that 'like' applies to qualities rather than to 'essence'.
So Basil after him in *Ep.* 8 (perhaps dependent on *de Syn.*), 360. "We in accord- "ance with the true doctrine speak of the Son as neither like, nor unlike the "Father. Each of these terms is equally impossible, for like and unlike are predi- "cated in relation to quality, and the divine is free from quality....We on the "contrary confess identity of nature and accept the one-ness of essence....For he "who is essentially God is of one essence with him who is essentially God." So it was that when the partial truth of "likeness" was put forward as the whole truth, the expression had to be abandoned. No form of likeness will really do. It would apply to some qualities and attributes perhaps: but in being God (that is in their οὐσία) Father and Son were not like but the same—of one οὐσία: in their special attributes and individual characteristics they were not like—they were distinct ὑποστάσεις.

of the 'Constantinopolitan' definition of the Faith, the champions of what we have called the new tradition maintain has been accepted and is current in the Catholic Church.

We pass on, therefore, to consider which doctrine it is that is to be attributed to the bishops and teachers to whose influence the final victory of the Homoi-ousian conception under the cloak of the Homo-ousian term is assigned.

And first of all the doctrine of Basil of Ancyra calls for consideration. It is his theology that Dr Harnack thinks was ultimately adopted, with some developments of their own, by the Cappadocians, Basil and the Gregories.

The position of Basil of Ancyra.

The position of Basil of Ancyra is fairly clear. It is first of all an attitude of opposition to the extreme development of Arian teaching represented by Aetius and Eunomius.

After the 'blasphemy of Sirmium' he presided at a counter-meeting at Ancyra (in 358) which anathematized everyone who did not faithfully confess the essential likeness of the Son to the Father, and in particular (with reference to numerous passages in the Gospel according to St John) all who so misinterpreted the sayings of Jesus as to conceive him to be "unlike" the Father[1]. The anathemas covered all the extreme Arian theses, and the emphatic declaration that the Son was like the Father even in *οὐσία* (i.e. in his very being) was at this juncture just the bridge that was needed to lead wanderers back to the Nicene faith in its fulness. By his action on this occasion the standpoint of Basil of Ancyra is to be determined. It is true the bridge broke down for the moment, because the 'moderates' went too far for the temper of the time by procuring sentences of exile against so many 'Anomoeans', whom the Emperor afterwards recalled. And so a deadlock resulted, and a compromise had to be found. And Basil joined in devising this compromise and had to sacrifice all reference to *οὐσία*, and (as one of the leaders of the conference held at Sirmium in May 359) agreed to the 'Dated' Creed[2]—the

[1] Hahn *Symbole*³ § 162.

[2] *ib.* § 163.

Creed which is unusually strong in its declarations on the eternal generation of the Son, but only says 'like the Father who begat him, according to the Scriptures' and 'like the Father in all things, as the holy Scriptures say and teach', and forbids all mention of the term substance (*οὐσία*) in reference to God, on the ground that though it was used in a simple or innocent sense by the fathers, yet it was not understood by the people and caused difficulties and was not contained in the Scriptures.

But though the stress of circumstances thus obliged him to consent to withdraw the disputed term from public and general—or at least from symbolical—use, he took pains at once to prepare a careful statement in defence of the doctrine for which it stood. In this[1] he declares that the formula *ὅμοιον κατὰ πάντα* really embraces everything and is enough to exclude any difference between Father and Son. He shews at length that though the term *οὐσία* is not contained in either the old or the new Scriptures, yet its sense is everywhere. He insists that the Son is not called the Word of God as being a mere force of expression or activity of utterance of God (*ἐνέργεια λεκτική*), but that as being Son he is also *οὐσία* (a definite entity), and so the fathers called him. He then goes on to argue against Arian or semi-Arian tenets; and, referring to the attempt to proscribe *οὐσία*, he says they wished to do away with the name *οὐσία* in order that, if it were no longer uttered by the mouth, their heresy might grow in the hearts of men. He suspects they will be caught writing 'like in will and purpose' but 'unlike in *οὐσία*'. But if they *bonâ fide* accept 'like in all things', then they gain nothing by getting rid of the term: for it makes the Son like the Father not only in regard to purpose and activity (*ἐνέργεια*) as they define it, but also in regard to his original being and his personal existence, and in regard to his very being as Son[2]. In a word, he declares, the formula 'in all things' includes absolutely everything and admits of no difference.

From such a statement as this it seems clear that *οὐσία* did

[1] Epiphanius *adv. Haer.* lxxiii 12—22 (esp. 15).

[2] *Ἔστιν ὅμοιος οὐ κατὰ τὴν βούλησιν καὶ τὴν ἐνέργειαν μόνην...ἀλλὰ κατὰ τὴν ὕπαρξιν καὶ κατὰ τὴν ὑπόστασιν καὶ κατὰ τὸ εἶναι ὡς Υἱός* (§ 15) and again *κατὰ τὸ εἶναι καὶ κατὰ τὸ ὑφεστάναι καὶ κατὰ τὸ ὑπάρχειν* (§ 22).

not mean to Basil anything like 'nature' or mere properties (which are represented rather by his phrases 'will' and 'activity' and 'purpose'), but real substantive being (*substantia*). Indeed he is so concerned to shew the fulness of the likeness that his statement runs some danger of proving too much. But it is just such a statement as Athanasius himself might have made, and did make, in similar circumstances[1].

To the statement put forward a little later by the Acacians at Seleucia, condemning alike the use of all the terms *ὁμοούσιον*, *ὁμοιούσιον*, and *ἀνόμοιον*, Basil did not agree, though forced by the Emperor later on to assent to and subscribe the Homoean Creed with 'in all things' omitted, when he went to Constantinople as one of the deputies from the synod[2].

That the really Homoean party were conscious that Basil's sympathies were not with them is shewn by the intrigues of Acacius and his friends against him—intrigues which resulted in his being banished on frivolous and unproved charges as soon as ever the Acacians had secured their influence over the Emperor Constantius[3].

If then it be the case that Basil of Ancyra is the father of the theology of the Cappadocians, Basil and the Gregories, it is a lineage of which they need not be ashamed.

But perhaps, although Basil of Ancyra may pass muster, the Meletians introduced the taint which has polluted the faith of the Church ever since. The position of Meletius and his followers must be considered next.

[1] It must be remembered also that Basil of Ancyra was expressly mentioned by Athanasius (*de Syn.* 41, written late in 359) among those who were really quite sound in the faith of Nicaea and only questioned the term *ὁμοούσιον*, towards whom he says 'we ought not to behave as though they were enemies...but we argue with them as brethren with brethren, since they have the same mind (*διάνοιαν*, i.e. mean the same thing) as ourselves...'.

[2] See the account of the sittings of the synod in Hefele *Councils* E. Tr. ii p. 264 ff.

[3] See Sozomen *H. E.* iv 24. He was deposed (along with Eustathius and Cyril of Jerusalem) as a set-off to the condemnation of Aetius, and he probably died in exile.

The sense in which Meletius and his party understood ὁμοούσιος.

The sense in which the Meletians at Constantinople accepted ὁμοούσιος must surely be determined by the gloss of Meletius himself when on a previous occasion—in view of the Emperor Jovian's declaration that he preferred the Homo-ousian doctrine to all others—he had at last brought himself (along with Acacius and twenty-five other bishops who wished to be on the winning side) to accept it. This was at a Synod held at Antioch in 363. The bishops present then formally signed and acknowledged the Nicene Creed, and further defined what they understood the term ὁμοούσιος to mean in the following words[1]: "The term therein "contained which is approved of (*al.* suspected) by some—to wit, "the term ὁμοούσιος—has received from the fathers a safe inter- "pretation, which shews that the Son was begotten from the "being (essence) of the Father, and that he is like the Father in "being (essence)."

It is true they proceed: "not indeed as though any passion "were thought of in regard to that ineffable generation, nor "according to any Grecian usage is the term οὐσία taken by the "Fathers, but for the refutation of the impious and daring "assertion of Arius concerning Christ, that he was 'out of "nothing' (out of that which was non-existent), which the modern "school of the Anomoeans yet more hardily and daringly proclaim "to the destruction of the concord of the Church."

And Hefele, so far agreeing with Harnack, says that by this gloss they 'left a loophole' for themselves and 'intended somewhat to weaken and semi-Arianise the expression ὁμοούσιος'.

But really it is clear that the gloss refers especially to the phrase ἐκ τῆς οὐσίας τοῦ πατρὸς...ἐγεννήθη: it is intended to guard the conception of generation and to exclude all materializing speculations. So that they are saying of the phrase ἐκ τῆς οὐσίας in effect precisely what Athanasius says—namely that it was intended to shew the meaning of 'begotten *of the Father*', and so

[1] Socrates *H. E.* iii 25, and Hefele *Councils* E. Tr. ii p. 282.

to exclude the conception that his origin was in any way external to the Father (which is what was meant by ἐξ οὐκ ὄντων).

We have, accordingly, here both ἐκ τῆς οὐσίας and ὅμοιος κατ' οὐσίαν: that is to say, ὁμοούσιος is accepted precisely in the terms which Athanasius declared to be an exact equivalent. If therefore their gloss was one that would have satisfied Athanasius, who is to object to it? Or at any rate how can it be said that they meant by it something other than ὁμοούσιος meant to the 'old Nicenes'? How, on such a point, can anyone today know better than Athanasius himself? And with such evidence before us, on what grounds are we to suppose that at the Council of Constantinople the term meant to Meletius only ὅμοιος κατ' οὐσίαν? When, for example, in the Creed ascribed to Damasus[1] we find 'non creatum sed genitum, non ex nihilo sed ex Patre, unius substantiae cum Patre' we do not suspect any Homoean or Arian intention.

Furthermore, at all events before the Council of 381, Meletius and his party had fully accepted the Western ('old-Nicene') interpretation of the Faith, and at a Synod held at Antioch had subscribed the pronouncements of the Church of Rome made in previous years on the questions at issue[2]. The effect of this is noted by Dr Harnack: "The triumph of the old-orthodox inter-"pretation of the Nicene Creed thus seemed perfect. The West, "under the guidance of Ambrose, from this time forth recognised "the Meletians as orthodox" (*DG.*[3] vol. ii p. 260 note, E. Tr. iv p. 93)[3].

[1] Hahn[3] p. 276.

[2] A hundred and forty-six oriental bishops were gathered there in September, 379 (the ninth month after the death of Basil). The Tome of Damasus concerning the synod of 378 was accepted (sc. the letter to Paulinus *Lat.* Hahn[3] p. 271 *Gk.* Thdt. *H. E.* v 11), and they also published a synodal letter of their own to the bishops of Italy and Gaul. See Hefele, *Councils*, ii p. 291. That the letter to Paulinus was one of the Roman statements accepted at Antioch in 379, and again that it was the 'Western tome' accepted at Constantinople, seems all but certain, in spite of some doubts that are felt about it. Cf. Harnack, *DG.*[3] vol. ii p. 269, note 1, E. Tr. iv p. 102, note 1, with Hefele *l. c.* and Ffoulkes, *D. C. A.* ii p. 1813.

[3] Yet Dr Harnack could write on the very next page that the reversal of the policy of Theodosius—viz. the transference of his support from the old orthodoxy to the new orthodoxy—was 'shewn most strikingly by the fact that Meletius of Antioch was called upon to preside at the Council, the very man who was specially

The acceptance of the Tome of Damasus at Antioch in 379 is really decisive—the eleventh anathema defines the meaning of 'natum de Patre' to be 'de substantia ipsius divina'.

But after all to Meletius personally, who died shortly after the Council met, no large share of responsibility for its decisions can be attributed. We rather want evidence of the real convictions of the bishops as a body who took part in it. We find this evidence in the letter which a year later they wrote in answer to an invitation to attend another Council to be held at Rome. In this letter[1] they believe themselves to be simply expressing a doctrine accordant with the decisions of the Councils of 379 and 381 (this is explicitly stated), and they proclaim their faith in the un-created co-essential co-eternal Trinity, insisting that the deity and power and essence (οὐσία) of the Father and of the Son and of the Holy Spirit is one, their dignity one in honour and their kingdom co-eternal, (existing) in three complete *hypostases* or three complete *persons* (ὑποστάσεσιν ἤγουν...προσώποις), while at the same time they repudiate any confusion of the *hypostases* or destruction of the individual characteristics, and equally any division of the essence or nature or deity (τῆς οὐσίας ἢ τῆς φύσεως ἢ τῆς θεότητος). Here, then, we have all the technical terms which have been before us, carefully used with due discrimination: οὐσία as the dominant word to express the being of the Godhead in itself, ὑπόστασις or πρόσωπον to express the particular mode of being in three persons, and φύσις to describe the characteristics common to all who share together in the one οὐσία.

Οὐσία does not here mean 'nature'. Nor does it in the controversies of the following half-century. In these Christological controversies indeed the discussions are about φύσις (natura) rather than about οὐσία (substantia); but φύσις does not really usurp the place of οὐσία. On the contrary φύσις tends to be used rather in the sense of 'person' (ὑπόστασις or πρόσωπον) —in accordance with the feeling that a complete 'nature' connoted a 'person'. Cyril's use of μία φύσις, however carefully guarded, shews the influence of this feeling and accounts for the suspicion

suspected by the orthodox of the West'—and this a full year after it must have been known to all concerned in the West that the Meletians had at last come round to the orthodox standpoint.

[1] Thdt. *H. E.* v 9.

which was widely entertained of Apollinarian tendencies in his thought[1].

So far, therefore, as the Meletians exercised influence on the Council of Constantinople, and as that influence can be traced, it was not in favour of any other doctrine than that for which the Nicenes had fought. Nor do the later controversies down to the time of Chalcedon furnish any proof of a change of mind as regards the main question now under consideration on the part of any considerable body in the Church.

The sense in which the Cappadocians understood ὁμοούσιος.

We must next examine the conceptions of the Cappadocians, and first and foremost of Basil, who as bishop of Caesarea from 370 to 379 was the head of the Cappadocian Churches. It is on Basil's presentation of the case that Dr Harnack depends for evidence in support of his theory. The evidence is drawn from the correspondence of Basil with Apollinarius. This correspondence, if genuine, is of the highest importance for the purpose of this investigation. It is necessary to examine it in detail[2].

[1] Cyril does not speak of *οὐσία*, and his frequent use of expressions like *καθ' ὑπόστασιν ἡνῶσθαι* (*ἕνωσις*) shews that by *ὑπόστασις* he means a *personal* existence. So Marius Mercator rendered it by the Latin *subsistentia* (e.g. Anathemas ii and iv), though once, apparently inaccurately, by *substantia* (Anathema iii).

On the other hand it would seem from the translation of Marius M. that Nestorius did use the term *οὐσία* (An. ii 'essentia') and probably also *ὑπόστασις*, but according to the older usage as equivalent to *οὐσία*, rightly rendered, therefore, by *substantia*.

[2] The correspondence was first discovered by Cotelier in a 'Harlaean' MS (see note p. 83) and published in 1681 (*Ecclesiae Graecae Monumenta* tom. 2). The only clear external evidence in favour of its genuineness was the heading of the letters in the MS in which they were found; while the (supposed) stainless orthodoxy of Basil made it seem improbable that he could ever have engaged in such friendly intercourse with the heretic Apollinarius; and the correspondence was at once condemned as spurious alike by Cotelier himself and by the Benedictines. Dr Dräseke however (*Texte u. Unters.* vii 3, 100 ff., 1892, where the letters are given, as they are also in Migne's edition of the letters of Basil, *Epp.* 361—364) has examined the matter in detail, and concludes his investigation with the strong assertion that 'there does not exist the slightest ground for not regarding the letters as genuine'. This conclusion might be admitted at once so far as the internal evidence of the letters is to be held decisive. There is nothing in them which might not have been written by Basil and Apollinarius respectively, say about the years 358–362, not to attempt at the moment a closer date. [I do not think Dräseke's dates

are quite consistent, nor should I accept his proposed emendations of κ′ and κε′ in *Epp.* 226, 224, as satisfactory: but the question of time would not be conclusive.] Apollinarius was at the height of his fame as a champion of the Nicene faith; it was most natural that Basil in his solitude should write to him, and this letter faithfully represents what we know from other sources to have been a common attitude at the time. I must emphasize the fact that there is nothing whatever original in it. Certainly no charge of being a pupil and follower of Apollinarius could properly lie against him merely on the strength of such a letter. That one person familiar with the writings of Basil and Apollinarius might have written all the letters seems to me certain, but the personal touches and details and the whole setting of the correspondence appear to forbid the assumption of forgery. What purpose would the forgery have served? And again there may be reckoned as further external evidence in favour of Dräseke's conclusion, (1) the fact that Ephraem Syrus appeals to a letter of Basil to Apollinarius in support of the doctrine that the Divine Logos suffered in the flesh (not in the divine nature), and (2) the credence given to the attacks made upon Basil on the ground of his intimate connexion with Apollinarius (attacks made after Apollinarius had developed his peculiar Christological doctrine). Dr Dräseke argues that such charges would never have carried weight unless it was known that there had been much closer relations and therefore more interchange of correspondence between them than Basil admits.

But though there is no internal evidence against the letters and some external evidence in their favour, I am myself entirely unable to set aside the strong external evidence against them which the admittedly genuine letters of Basil furnish, and I do not think that Dr Dräseke's attempts to explain away the statements in detail have in any degree weakened the cumulative force of the general effect of Basil's declarations.

There is first (though last in time) the general statement of the case in *Ep.* 244 to Bp Patrophilus (A.D. 376). Basil has read some—only a few—of the many writings of Apollinarius, and he sees reasons for honouring him rather for regarding him as an enemy. It is true he could find some things to censure in the writings he has read, but he is not in any respect either his teacher or his pupil, and he does not consider that he is responsible for anything Apollinarius or anyone else writes that others do not like.

But besides this general statement and disclaimer of the principle that he is to be made responsible for anyone else's opinions, Basil three times over faces the charge that he belongs to the school of A. and repels it in detail.

In *Ep.* 131 to Olympius (A.D. 373) he says that supposing he did sometime *many years ago* write to Apollinarius or anyone else, it cannot be made a reproach against him: he is not of his school or communion. It is for his own sins only that each man must die.

Again in *Ep.* 226 to his monks (A.D. 375), he says he is not to be judged by the words of any other, but by his own words. No one can bring as evidence against him the letters which *he wrote twenty years ago*, so as to prove from them that he still has connexion with the men who have since then written what is regarded as heretical. What he wrote then he wrote before anyone had raised any suspicion against the people in question; *as layman to laymen*; and moreover *nothing concerning the faith*, but only simple greetings such as met the obligations of friendly intercourse.

And yet again, in *Ep.* 224, to the presbyter Genethlios (in the same year A.D. 375), he insists that his opponents must prove definite acts of ecclesiastical communion on his part with Apollinarius or his clergy, if the charge against him is to lie. Whereas, he says, all that they have to shew is *a letter* written *five and twenty years ago as layman to a layman, on a chance occasion without premeditation, absolutely nothing whatever about the faith,* but simply a letter with friendly greetings (and even that not as he wrote it but tampered with--he knows not by whom).

Dr Dräseke emphasises the difference between the reference here to 'a letter' and the reference in *Ep.* 226 to 'letters': but it must be noted that in *Ep.* 226 the reference is much more general—not only are there letters (plural) but there are laymen (plural) to whom they are written (Basil would apparently include with the one letter written to Apollinarius other letters written at that time to other persons who might since then have incurred similar suspicion). The more exact reference in *Ep.* 224 must determine the sense of the more general statement in *Ep.* 226.

Dr Dräseke also supposes that by the phrase 'as layman to layman' Basil only means to describe the general tone and character of the letter as written with no sense of ecclesiastical responsibility, having no episcopal authority, and being entirely unofficial. It is true that Basil deprecates blaming a bishop for his casual writings as a layman, but, explained as the phrase is by the context 'nothing concerning the faith', the very least it can mean is that the letter in question was untechnical. And who will venture to say that such a description applies to the letters before us now? Not even, I think, Dr Dräseke's layman of old. Certainly not the trained theologian of to-day. It must further be noted that the opening words of the first of these letters refer to a previous interchange of letters concerning obscure things in the Scriptures, so that the acceptance of it carries also the acceptance of a whole series of letters which are not otherwise known to us. How, then, could Basil write as he does?

I leave out of court the idea that Basil again and again deliberately lied: and here there could clearly be no room for the practice of any 'economy' of the truth.

We are forced then to the conclusion that *either* Basil's memory played him false when he thought it was most precise, in regard to a matter of grave importance in which his honour and reputation were at stake—not on any sudden emergency, but again and again after full time for reflexion: *or* the original verdict on the letters discovered by Cotelier was just, and no such letters ever passed between Apollinarius and Basil.

In the absence of more conclusive evidence I choose the latter alternative.

But though I would not use this correspondence in support of the argument of this thesis, I am well content that the new reading of the history should rest upon it: so conclusively does it seem, if genuine, to tell against the new and in favour of the old historical tradition. At the time at which it is supposed to have been written Apollinarius was regarded as the foremost champion of the Nicene theology in the East, and the mere fact that it is he whom Basil chooses out as the expert theologian to whom to appeal is enough to shew that, far from starting from the Homoi-ousian standpoint, Basil is on the main question Nicene to the core, and simply wanted to see his way to answering the objections which were commonly urged from the opposite side against οὐσία and ὁμοούσιος.

The correspondence opens with a letter in which Basil appeals to Apollinarius for guidance on a matter which he feels to be of great importance.

"Those who have thrown everything into confusion and filled the "world with words and disputes have cast out the term οὐσία, as being "foreign to the scriptures. Be so good as to tell me in what sense the "fathers used it, and whether you have never found it anywhere in "scripture: for they will not allow that ἐπιούσιος ἄρτος and λαὸς "περιούσιος and any such phrases are at all relevant. Next, in regard "to ὁμοούσιος itself (for I am sure that the attack on οὐσία is designed "to cut the ground from under ὁμοούσιος), please tell me with some "fulness, what its meaning is, and how it can be soundly predicated in "cases in which (*a*) there is no common *genus* covering, (*b*) no material "*substratum* preexisting, (*c*) no partition of the first into the second. "I would have you fully set forth how we can call the Son ὁμοούσιος "with the Father, and yet not fall into any of these three conceptions. "I have imagined that whatever may be held to be fundamentally (καθ' "ὑπόθεσιν)[1] οὐσία of the Father, that must the οὐσία of the Son also of "necessity be held to be. For example, should a man call the οὐσία of "the Father 'light intelligible everlasting ingenerate', he will call the "οὐσία of the Son also 'light intelligible everlasting generate'. Now "to express this conception it seems to me that the term ἀπαραλλάκτως "ὅμοιος ('like without any variation') is better suited than the term "ὁμοούσιος. For of light and light, where there is no difference of more "and less, I fancy we should be right in saying, not that the one is the "same as the other—because each exists in a circumscription of the "οὐσία which is its own—but that one is like the other in respect of "οὐσία, exactly and without variation (ὅμοιον δὲ κατ' οὐσίαν ἀκριβῶς καὶ "ἀπαραλλάκτως)." In conclusion he declares that he has opened his heart, and he begs that he may be treated by the physician's skill.

[1] καθ' ὑπόθεσιν—perh. *ex hypothesi*, 'according to the particular supposition', 'for the sake of argument', 'as assumed'. So regularly used, as e.g. by Basil himself, *adv. Ennom.* i 19—a passage so similar in thought and language to this that, if the letter be not genuine, it might have furnished the materials for its chief contents. But ὑπόθεσις (which is always passive) is also commonly used to express the 'basis' or 'foundation' of actions or states or conditions of things, and so might very well mean what ὑπόστασις (itself the recognised passive form of the verbal of ὑποτίθημι) originally expressed, i.e. the underlying principle or essence or *substratum*. "Apollinarius" with "Basil's" letter open before him uses ὑπόθεσις thus (ἡ πάντων ἀνθρώπων ὑπόθεσις). And so, though I do not recall any other example of this sense, I would render "fundamentally" or "in its underlying essence".

This letter shews a keen appreciation of the points of controversy. It may be well at once to emphasise the point from which Basil clearly starts. As Apollinarius says at the outset of his reply, his belief is a godly one and his question is put with a nice discrimination (φιλοθέως πιστεύεις καὶ φιλολόγως ζητεῖς). He is accustomed to the terms *οὐσία* and *ὁμοούσιος*, which he accepts so far as he understands them. But he is aware (as everyone was) that various objections, difficult to meet, were urged against them. He mentions first the Scriptural objection, that the words were not to be found in the inspired writings of apostles and evangelists; and then he goes on to the philosophical objections, that the words implied (1) the existence of some *γένος* in which Father and Son were included, or (2) the existence of some *οὐσία* (identified with *εἶδος* or *ὕλη*) prior both to Father and to Son, which they shared in common and from which they were derived, or (3) a materialistic conception which would make Father and Son as it were parts or pieces of one *οὐσία*. These are the 'stock' objections, brought by every controversialist at the time[1].

Basil evinces no tendency to reject either *οὐσία* or *ὁμοούσιος*. Though disposed for his own part, in view of the difficulties, to use some other expression, he clearly believes that *ὁμοούσιος* is the right term to describe the relation between the Father and the Son, and he is only anxious to be shewn how he can use the term without getting involved in the difficulties which he mentions. He wants, that is, to have a safe way of stating the relation: biblical authority if possible, but at any rate dialectic or philosophic immunity.

The reply of Apollinarius on the points submitted to him is as follows:

"One *οὐσία* is not predicated only where there is numerical unity, "as you (rightly) say, and where[2] what is in question is contained by "a single circumscription; but also, in a proper sense, in the case of "two men or whatever instance may be taken of things united in

[1] For other answers to them than those of Apollinarius see Athanasius *de Decr.* 18, 20; *Or. c. Ar.* i 14; *de Syn.* 51; Hilary *de Syn.* 68.

[2] Reading τῷ ἐν μιᾷ περιγραφῇ for τὸ ἐν μ. π. —a common confusion in MSS (περιγραφή, the 'limit-line' of 'individual' existence).

"respect of *γένος*. In this way not only two but more things[1] can be "the same in respect of their *οὐσία*: even as all we men are Adam, "seeing that we are one (man); and the son of David is David, as "being the same as he: just as further you rightly say that the Son is "in respect of his *οὐσία* that which the Father is; for in no other way "could the Son be God, since the Father is confessed to be the one and "only God; as indeed there is one Adam the beginner of the *γένος* of "men, and one David the founder of the royal *γένος*. In this way, "I think, we shall be saved from supposing that there is one *γένος* "covering or one *ὕλη* underlying in the case of Father and Son, when "we compare[2] the property of the ultimate *ἀρχή* as beginner of a *γένος* "and the *γένη* which proceed from the beginners of *γένη* with the only "begotten offspring (*μονογενὲς γέννημα*) of the one *ἀρχή*. For such as "these (viz. *γένη* and *ἀρχαί*) do come to some extent into the category "of likeness, in a way which does not apply even in the case of Adam, "who was formed by God, and ourselves, who are begotten of man: "for in our case there is neither one covering *γένος* (but the *ἀρχή* of "men is Adam himself), nor is there a *ὕλη* common to him and us "(but he himself is the *substratum* of all men); nor surely is there a "previous conception of David and the *γένος* of David, in so far as "David (in that the peculiar characteristic of David begins with[3] "David) is himself the *substratum* of all who spring from him[4]. Yet, "since these instances are inadequate, in so far as there are different "relations in common between all men, as for example the relation of "brotherhood; in the instance of Father and Son I say there is nothing "of the kind—but the whole case is stated when you say the Father is "the *ἀρχή* and the Son is derived from the *ἀρχή*. There is thus neither

[1] Reading *πλείονα*, apparently with the MS.

[2] Reading *παραβάλωμεν* for *παραλάβωμεν*—also a very common confusion. This passage is rather obscure, but the line of thought seems to be as follows: He has taken three 'couples'—the Son and the Father, men and Adam, David's son and David: and he says the relation between the members of each of these couples is analogous; the *οὐσία* in each case is one. To this one *οὐσία* we refer both members alike, and we exclude from our minds any idea of a comprehensive genus including them, or of a common 'matter' in which they respectively share. To things which do come under the idea of a genus, or which do share a common matter, the predicate 'likeness' could be to some extent applied: but to the cases in view it cannot with any exactitude be applied at all.

[3] Reading *ἄρχεται* with Migne. Dräseke prints *ἔρχεται* 'comes from'.

[4] That is to say—and so there could be no previous 'David', in which he and they alike could share. And the writer goes on to maintain that still less does the idea of likeness apply to the Father and the Son.

"partition of the former into the latter, as in the case of bodies (which "might be divided)—but there is a generative act: nor yet is there a "partition as it were of the special characteristic of the Father into "the Son, but the special characteristic of the Son is plainly derived "from the Father's—the same in difference and different in sameness "(just as the Father is said to be in the Son and the Son in the "Father).

"It is true the difference will not in itself safeguard the reality of "the Sonship, nor on the other hand the sameness the indivisibility "of the ὑπόστασις[1]; but each is conjoint and one in εἶδος, the same "under different conditions and different under the same conditions[2]. "This prevents anyone unduly straining the expressions which are not "adequate to convey the meaning—even as the Lord gave us authority "for the conception when he represented the Father as greater while "being on a level and the Son as enjoying equality while being of lower "degree. And this taught us to conceive of the Son as in light of the "same form (εἶδος) but 'inferior', not changing the οὐσία but regarding "it as at once (i.e. while one and the same) superior and in a state of "inferiority. For those who accept the term οὐσία without at all recog- "nising its sameness bring in the idea of 'likeness' which has nothing "to do with the matter and apply it to the Son: 'likeness' I say—a "conception which extends even to men who are 'made like' to God[3]. "But those who know that 'likeness' is a conception that rather befits "things made, connect the Son with the Father in 'a sameness'—but a "sameness of lower grade, that he may not be the Father himself or a "portion of the Father—truths which the phrase 'the Son is other' "strongly attest[4]. In this way he is God, not as being the Father, but "as being from the Father; not the original, but the image. He is in "this way ὁμοούσιος in a wholly special and peculiar sense, not as things "that are of the same γένος (ὁμογενῆ), not as things that are parted off "from something, but as being the one and only offspring of the one "γένος and εἶδος Deity, by an indivisible and incorporeal process, in ac-

[1] Apparently used as οὐσία—the entity, the substantia.

[2] I.e. the same in οὐσία (God), but existing in different modes or spheres; different as regards sphere or function, but always as God the same.

[3] I.e. and therefore a conception which must be inadequate to express the relation between the Son and the Father—the Son being on an entirely different plane, having the οὐσία God, whereas men have the οὐσία man.

[4] Reading τὸ instead of τῷ. For the phrase 'the Son is other' cf. Tertullian *adv. Prax.* § 9, cited *supra* p. 20.

"cordance with which that which generates, while still remaining in its "ingenerate individuality, proceeded into the generate individuality[1]."

This letter, for all its occasional obscurity in detail, is undoubtedly an able statement of the case, and the significance of the answer to Basil's questions is unmistakable. Apollinarius assures him that *ὁμοούσιος* is a more correct and better term to use than the form of words which he suggested in its stead, and that properly understood it is free from any of the objectionable meanings which he feared. The Son, he declares, is related to the Father as men to Adam. Just as it can be said of all men that they are Adam, for all are one; and just as there is only one Adam: so it is also in the case of the Godhead. That is to say—though he does not use the actual words: As men are *ὁμοούσιοι* with Adam: so the Son is *ὁμοούσιος* with the Father. Thus Apollinarius clearly conceives of the unity of the human race and the unity of the Godhead as analogous: in each case the *οὐσία* is one and the same. And the warning which he gives Basil against the notion of 'likeness', in regard to the relation between the Father and the Son, he emphasises much more strongly in a second letter. Likeness describes the relation of a statue to a king. He will not tolerate the phrase *ὅμοιος κατ' οὐσίαν* as a substitute for *ὁμοούσιος*: it is, he says, lacking in discrimination of terminology and prompted by an evil intention (*χυδαίως ὀνομασθὲν καὶ κακοήθως νοηθέν*); whereas *ὁμοούσιος* signifies that the Son is 'not *like* God, but God', a genuine offspring and of the same *οὐσία* with him of whom he is the offspring.

[1] The text is uncertain. I translate *καθ' ἣν μένον τὸ γεννῶν ἐν τῇ ἀγεννήτῳ ἰδιότητι προῆλθεν εἰς τὴν γεννητὴν ἰδιότητα*. (Migne's *μόνον* is doubtless a misprint; *γεννητὴν* is Cotelier's emendation of the MS *γεννητικήν*.) 'Ἰδιότης means the individual characteristics, the 'mode of being', that which characterises each *ὑπόστασις* of Deity. So we have here the familiar idea that God, ingenerate as Father, becomes generate as Son, but by becoming generate as Son does not in any way lose the ingenerate characteristics which attach to Deity as Father (cf. the similar conception that the Son in becoming Man always remains what he was as God).

The MS *γεννητικήν* would however be possible, expressing a rather different thought. The ingenerate God may become generative (may generate) without undergoing any alteration of his ingenerate Deity (this in view of a common Arian argument against the idea of Sonship in the Godhead altogether, on the ground that the idea of generation involved change, and change could not be thought of in regard to Deity).

The correspondence, therefore, if its genuineness be admitted, by no means shews that Basil started from the homoi-ousian standpoint, and was satisfied with a generic unity[1] of Father and Son. On the contrary, it is obvious that as to the very core of the question at issue Basil is Nicene of the Nicenes. He starts with the conviction that the real underlying essential being (the *οὐσία*) of Father and Son, whatever it is, is one and the same. It is only because of the 'individual' existence of the *οὐσία* in each that he thinks it would be better to say that they are *ὅμοιοι κατ' οὐσίαν ἀκριβῶς καὶ ἀπαραλλάκτως*; and he only makes the suggestion tentatively, desiring more light upon the question, and willing to be corrected. That he was conscious of a difference of meaning between *ὁμοούσιος* and *ὁμοιούσιος* is surely certain.

And his own words elsewhere remove any doubt that might be felt about the fact. He says[2] "If *invariably* is conjoined to "*like in essence* I accept the phrase as conveying the same sense "as *homo-ousios*, according to the sound meaning of homo-"ousios...but if anyone cuts off *invariably* from *like*...I suspect "the term as belittling the glory of the Only begotten." The addition of 'invariably', *ἀπαραλλάκτως*, seems to mark that the *οὐσία* undergoes no kind of change in the act of eternal generation, but is all along the same in the Son as in the Father: and indeed Basil says almost as much in this connexion. "Being of this "mind" he writes "the fathers at Nicaea spoke of the Only "begotten as *Light of Light, Very God of very God*, and so on, "and then consistently added *of the same essence.* It is impossible "for any one to entertain the idea of variableness of light in "relation to light (this is obviously to say light is always light—"there is one *οὐσία* light, so one *οὐσία* God), of truth in relation

[1] Harnack emphasises this point. But it really seems quite clear that it is not the unity of a genus (i.e. of many members of one genus) that is the controlling thought. It is rather this—there is one *οὐσία* Godhead, and the Son has that *οὐσία* just as the Father has: and (for illustration) there is one *οὐσία* Manhood—the type and embodiment of which is Adam, and all men have that *οὐσία* just as Adam has it. So the stress is on the oneness of the *οὐσία*, *substantia*, rather than on the union of those that have it—the *genus*.

[2] *Ep.* 9. The letter is supposed to have been written in 360; v. Gwatkin *Studies of Arianism* p. 242, note 3.

"to truth, or of the essence of the Only begotten in relation to "that of the Father. If, then, the phrase be accepted in this "sense, I have no objection to it." Here then we have Basil, while accepting ὁμοούσιος as in itself decisive and unequivocal, willing to recognise the orthodoxy of those who, shrinking from the actual term, maintained instead what he regarded as equivalent in sense—ἀπαραλλάκτως ὁμοιούσιος. In this he is but following in the steps of Athanasius himself—anxious, as he had been, for the sense rather than the words. Just in this spirit, the spirit of comprehension, which, without any sacrifice of belief, would embrace all who agreed in thought however divided they might seem to be in expression, Athanasius had declared that those who said *both ὁμοιούσιος and ἐκ τῆς οὐσίας* were really saying ὁμοούσιος though they rejected the term. "While any one who "says only *like-in-essence* does certainly not declare at the same "time *of the essence*, yet he who says *one-in-essence* signifies the "sense of the two terms *like-in-essence* and *of the essence* both "together[1]." The explanation Basil gives of the significance of the addition ἀπαραλλάκτως to ὁμοιούσιος shews that he means by it what Athanasius meant by ἐκ τῆς οὐσίας in the same connexion. Had they discussed this particular question together, as a similar question was discussed at the council held by Athanasius in 362, it seems certain that they would have found themselves in close agreement as to the real value of each other's terms[2].

[1] Athanasius *de Syn.* 41.

[2] Indeed Athanasius insists that unchangeable likeness means the same as ὁμοούσιος, both in the *de Decr.* 20, cf. 24, where he argues for the term ὁμοούσιος (saying the bishops at Nicaea used it in order to shew that the Son was not only like but ταὐτὸν τῇ ὁμοιώσει ἐκ τοῦ πατρός, and that ἡ τοῦ υἱοῦ ὁμοίωσις καὶ ἀτρεψία was *sui generis*—not as men may be 'like' by observance of commands and virtue), and also more precisely in the first *Oratio c. Ar.* § 22, when avoiding all use of the disputed term he directs his argument to shew—as sufficient in itself—that the Son is the unalterable image of the Father (it being admitted that he is 'image' and ἐκ τοῦ πατρός, it follows necessarily that he remains what he is and is not changed—μένων ὅ ἐστι καὶ οὐκ ἀλλασσόμενος...ἐξ ἀνάγκης καὶ εἰκὼν ὅ ἐστι διαμένει καὶ οὐ τραπήσεται). There can only be 'unchangeable likeness', an 'unalterable image', when the οὐσία is one and the same. The phraseology is strictly parallel with Basil's τὸ ἄτρεπτον τῆς οὐσίας *de Spiritu S.* § 48.

Harnack, it is true, speaks of the signal reserve of Athanasius towards Basil and pictures a state of tension between them. But in the letters which have been preserved from Basil to him (Basil *Epp.* 61, 66, 68, 69, 80, 82) I find no trace on

But in any case even if Basil's ἀπαραλλάκτως does not cover all the significance of ἐκ τῆς οὐσίας, it is for the use of others that he vindicates the phrase. He has no need of any formula of comprehension for himself. For himself ὁμοούσιος is the term at hand.

And here must be noted a very curious reading of the argument of Athanasius. Dr Harnack[1] adopts in effect an algebraical process and says that if, as Athanasius declares,

ὁμοιούσιος + ἐκ τῆς οὐσίας = ὁμοούσιος,
∴ ὁμοούσιος − ἐκ τῆς οὐσίας = ὁμοιούσιος.

The true inference from the argument of Athanasius is, that though if you say ὁμοιούσιος you must add ἐκ τῆς οὐσίας in order to have 'a sound form of words', yet if you say ὁμοούσιος you

Basil's part of anything but highest esteem and desire to follow his guidance: though he is anxious for the absolute repudiation of Marcellus, which could never be elicited from Athanasius; and though the council Basil longed for was not summoned—but that was not the fault of Athanasius. See too the reference to him in *Ep.* 204, as one whose judgment must be accepted. And certainly on Basil's election as bishop Athanasius wrote hearty congratulations. He praises Basil in the warmest terms and will hear nothing against him when busybodies find fault with him. To two of these he writes: "I have been utterly astonished "at the boldness of those who venture to speak against our beloved Basil the "bishop, a true servant of God: for from such vain talk they can be convicted of "not loving even the confession of the fathers" (*Ep.* 62 to John and Antiochus). And to another, a presbyter of Caesarea, he says: "Whereas you have told me of "the monks at Caesarea...that they are vexed and are opposing our beloved bishop "Basil, I am glad you have informed me, and I have pointed out to them what is "fitting, namely that as children they should obey their father, and not oppose "what he approves. For if he were suspected as touching the truth, they would do "well to combat him. But if they are confident, as we all are, that he is a glory to "the Church, contending rather on behalf of the truth and teaching those who "require it, it is not right to combat such an one, but rather to accept with thanks "his good conscience. For...they appear to be vexed without cause. For he, as I "am confident, to the weak becomes weak, to gain the weak (1 Cor. ix 22). But let "our beloved friends look at the scope of his truth, and at his special purpose, and "glorify the Lord who has given such a bishop to Cappadocia as any district must "pray to have" (*Ep.* 63 to the presbyter Palladius). The special attack upon Basil which is in view in these letters was in regard to the doctrine of the Holy Spirit rather than the doctrine of the Son; but his most exacting admirer could hardly ask for fuller recognition of his merits and warmer support than Athanasius bestows. There is at least no indication of distrust or reserve.

[1] *DG.*[3] vol. ii p. 266, E. Tr. vol. iv p. 99, the passage cited *supra* p. 9.

need add nothing at all. Every other term needs qualification and amplification and explanation. Homo-ousios by itself is sufficient and decisive. It is difficult to conceive how the words of Athanasius can be understood to lead to such a conclusion as is embodied in the above equations. It would indeed have been strange if expert theologians, intending—after so long a controversy—to accept ὁμοούσιος and reject ὁμοιούσιος, strained out the term and swallowed the sense. At least we want some clear and certain proof that they did.

That the mere absence of ἐκ τῆς οὐσίας is without dogmatic significance will be further shewn later on[1].

There remains only to be considered the possibility, hinted at rather than expressed by Dr Harnack, that οὐσία meant to Basil something so different from what it meant to Athanasius, that Basil's ὁμοούσιος meant what Athanasius understood by ὁμοιούσιος[2]. These two points then still require examination. First, what did Basil mean by οὐσία? Secondly, does ὁμοούσιος with him become what ὁμοιούσιος was to Athanasius? The answer to the second question will not necessarily be *yes*, even if it is found that οὐσία is used in a somewhat different sense.

What οὐσία (and ὁμοούσιος) meant to Basil.

Basil clearly distinguishes οὐσία from its attributes in thought at least, e.g. when (in regard to the contention of the Eunomians and their inductions from τὸ ἀγέννητον) he declares that the οὐσία of God is αὐτὸ τὸ εἶναι τοῦ θεοῦ (*adv. Eunom.* i 10) and must not be identified with what is merely characteristic. So again (*ib.* i 19), in regard to the meaning of the community of οὐσία between the persons (τὸ τῆς οὐσίας κοινόν), he says it should be taken to denote that the λόγος τοῦ εἶναι of each is one and the same. He does not say the φύσις—it would not be enough to say the φύσις. So that, to take an example, if you say the Father is τῷ ὑποκειμένῳ Light, you will also say that the οὐσία of the Only-begotten is Light too. The difference exists in number and

[1] See *infra* p. 59.
[2] This is definitely maintained by Zahn, pp. 21, 87.

in the special properties which characterise each of the two; but the unity is contemplated ἐν τῷ λόγῳ τῆς θεότητος. (Cf. *Ep.* 236. 6 quoted *infra.*)

Instances of his usage of the term οὐσία may be taken almost at random from his writings. E.g. *adv. Eunom.* ii 4, in connexion with the analogy 'Peter and Paul' he defines οὐσία as τὸ ὑλικὸν ὑποκείμενον (the 'substantial' subject) and distinguishes it from the ἰδιώματα—ἰδιότητες αἳ τὸ καθ' ἕνα χαρακτηρίζουσιν—the χαρακτῆρες of individual forms of existence of the one οὐσία. So, again, *ib.* ii 9 he distinguishes between (1) 'names' which are indicative of πράγματα ὑποκείμενα αὐτοῖς—such as man, horse, ox; and (2) 'names' which only shew τὴν σχέσιν (relation)—such as son, slave, friend; and pronounces that the latter cannot be described by the term οὐσία.

In the discussion in regard to the Godhead he is, of course, most concerned to mark off that which there is in common, which is indicated by the term οὐσία, from that which is particular, which is indicated by the terms ἰδιώματα, ὑπόστασις. But though the common οὐσία Divinity includes the nature of Divinity which is also common to the Three, yet it is logically to be distinguished from it. It is not its nature.

Nevertheless in distinguishing between the ὑποστάσεις (or the ἰδιώματα) it is usually enough for his purpose to emphasize the 'nature' as that which is common; and this is frequently his practice, as in his treatise on the Holy Spirit (e.g. § 45 κατὰ μὲν τὴν ἰδιότητα τῶν προσώπων εἷς καὶ εἷς, κατὰ δὲ τὸ κοινὸν τῆς φύσεως ἓν οἱ ἀμφότεροι), though whenever the idea of οὐσία rather than φύσις is required the word is at once forthcoming, e.g. §§ 19, 41. The main idea of Basil, as of the other Cappadocians, is that the οὐσία of the Godhead cannot be understood, but that its attributes and 'nature' may be known from revelation; and this being so they speak more readily of the φύσις, which can be known in some measure, as that in which the community of life in the Holy Trinity consists. (Cf. Basil *adv. Eunom.* i §§ 13, 14; *Hexaem.* i § 8 on Is. xl. 22, warning against the attempt to find out what οὐσία is, or to search for a nature void of qualities. And see in this connexion Aristotle *Met.* vii 3 of cases in which οὐκ ἔστι τὸ τί ἔστιν ὁρίσασθαι...ἀλλὰ ποῖον μὲν τί ἐστιν ἐνδέχεται καὶ διδάξαι.)

So when he repels arguments as to number on the ground that number relates to quantity, which is not applicable to God, he says "we confess one God not in number but in nature" (*Ep.* 8); and he goes on in the same spirit to declare 'like' and 'unlike' equally unsuitable terms to express the relation of the Son to the Father, inasmuch as they are predicated in relation to quality and the divine is free from quality. "We", he says, "on the contrary confess identity of nature (*ταὐτότητα τῆς* "*φύσεως*) and accept the oneness of essence (*τὸ ὁμοούσιον*)"— a collocation in which *οὐσία* and *φύσις* are sufficiently distinguished.

So too in the letter to his brother Gregory (*Ep.* 38), when he sets himself to expound the difference between *οὐσία* and *ὑπόστασις*, and declares that *οὐσία* is that which is common (*κοινόν*), which several can have at the same time, while *ὑπόστασις* is that which is individual (*ἴδιον*), which marks off one from another[1]; he writes *currente calamo* of the *κοινότης τῆς φύσεως* (*τὸ κοινὸν τῆς φύσεως*), but then immediately afterwards uses *οὐσία* and *ὁμοούσιον* (§ 2). He distinguishes the indefinite (general) notion of *οὐσία* from the particular form of it *ὑπόστασις*, but at the same time contrasts *τὴν μὲν φύσιν* and *τὸ δὲ ὑφεστός*—'man' the *φύσις* and 'Paul' the *φύσις ὑφεστῶσα* (§ 3). And then (§ 4) again he finds the *κοινότης τῆς οὐσίας* the readiest mode of expression, and combines the two terms *οὐσία* and *φύσις* in a single sentence declaring that the union (*κοινωνία*) and the distinction are alike indescribable and inconceivable—"the difference of the *ὑποστάσεις* not interrupting the "continuity of the nature, and the *κοινότης* in respect of *οὐσία* "not confusing the individuality of the characteristics."

At another time, in similar connexions, discriminating the *κοινόν* and the *ἴδιον*, he uses *οὐσία* of the former all through (*Ep.* 214); and yet again (*Ep.* 52) the term employed is *φύσις*.

There is however no justification for the assertion that the terms are identical. *Φύσις* will often express all that is needed: that is the only true inference that can be drawn. That *οὐσία* retained its proper meaning is shewn in another instance (*Ep.*

[1] See additional note on *ὑπόστασις* p. 81 *infra*.

236. 6)—"We confess one οὐσία in regard to the Godhead, so as "not to explain (or define) in different ways its existence (ὥστε "τὸν τοῦ εἶναι λόγον μὴ διαφόρως ἀποδιδόναι)"; but at the same time we confess "a particular hypostasis", since it is not enough to "form our conception of God from the general idea of existence", but we must have a distinct perception of the separate characteristics[1].

It is true, as Zahn says, that Basil is never tired of proclaiming the difference between the two expressions οὐσία and ὑπόστασις, and that his zeal for the distinction carried him so far as to lead him to assert that the Nicene fathers were fully alive to the difference (*Ep.* 125).

But, though Basil was doubtless wrong on this latter point, Zahn puts the case against him in somewhat misleading fashion when he says (p. 88) that as a matter of fact the use of both terms without distinction had been sanctioned at Alexandria shortly before Basil wrote. As a matter of fact the account of Athanasius (*Tom. ad Antiochenos*) shews that the term ὑπόστασις only was under consideration; and that, though it was found that those who said 'one hypostasis' and those who said 'three hypostases' really agreed in their belief (when closely examined as to meaning apart from terms), and so that both expressions could be used in a pious sense; yet it was decided that the terms were open to misunderstanding, and both sides agreed to give up using them and to be content with the expression of the faith contained in the Creed of Nicaea (i.e., evidently, not to speak either of 'one hypostasis' or of 'three hypostases', but to use the words of the Creed—the anathema was not apparently referred to). On the other hand the distinction which Basil 'is never tired of proclaiming' is so obviously convenient, that it must be counted all to his credit that he succeeded in winning currency for it.

Again, if Tertullian's epigrammatic phrase (*de Anima* 32)—'nature' makes partners (*communicat*), while 'substance' sets apart (*discordat*)—be borne in mind, it might seem that when Basil declares that οὐσία signifies the κοινόν and ὑπόστασις the ἴδιον (*Ep.* 214. 4 et passim) he is no longer using οὐσία in the sense in which Tertullian used *substantia*, but rather (as Harnack and Zahn suggest) in the sense of *natura*, and so not in the Nicene sense. But the contradiction is only apparent. Tertullian, in this passage, has not the Godhead—the Trinity—in view.

[1] Cf. also *Hexaem.* vi 3 "We distinguish substance susceptible of quality and the quality which it receives."

That he held the Three to be one in substance is perfectly certain, and as regards the Trinity both the *substantia* and the *natura* were the same and unique (see passages cited *supra*). On the other hand, Basil certainly has not in view any distinction between the being (substance) and the nature, nor is he thinking of the *nature* as that which was common to the three and the *substance* as that which was peculiar to each, marking off one from another[1]. He is only trying to find—or to get accepted—two terms that will clearly express two distinct conceptions, so that one can stand for Godhead in its being and nature and all that belongs essentially to it (so that Godhead is not there if *it* is not there), while the other will express the different forms in which the same Godhead and nature exists.

And it is an equally unguarded account of Basil's teaching to say that in a dogmatic letter to his brother Gregory (*Ep.* 38) he is content to explain the conception of the ὁμοουσία as meaning unity of disposition such as existed between Paul and Timothy (Zahn p. 87)[2].

The position of Basil in regard to the meaning of οὐσία seems to be well put in the following summary of part of his argument against Eunomius:

"The main contention of Basil against Eunomius is that the "word unbegotten is not a name indicative of the being of God, "but only of a mode of existence (ὑπάρξεως τρόπος τὸ ἀγέννητον "καὶ οὐκ οὐσίας ὄνομα, *adv. Eunom.* iv p. 763 C). The divine "being has other predicates. If every peculiar mode of existence "involves a distinction in being also, and if the Son cannot be of "the like being (essence) with the Father, because He has a peculiar "mode of existence and the Father another; men cannot be of "like being, because each of them represents a different mode of "existence. By the names of Father, Son, and Spirit, we do not "understand different essences (οὐσίαι), but they are names which "distinguish the ὕπαρξις of each of them (p. 765 B). All are God, "and so the Father cannot be more God than the Son, as one man

[1] The contention that Basil uses 'substance' as Tertullian used 'nature' might thus be disproved at once by the method of *reductio ad absurdum*. It is also clear that if οὐσία does not mean to Basil what it had meant to Athanasius (viz. what *substantia* meant to Tertullian), then Basil has no word at all to express the *being* of the Godhead as distinguished from its *nature*. But the passages cited *supra* entirely forbid the suggestion.

[2] Cf. p. 55.

"is no more man than another. Quantitative differences are not "reckoned in regard to essence; the question is only of being or "non-being. But this does not exclude the idea of a variety in "being in the Son and the Father (ἑτέρως ἔχειν p. 762)—the "generation of the former. Both must have equal dignity, for "the essence of Begetter and Begotten must be the same, and "that which is caused is not always less than the cause (761 B)." Dorner, *Geschichte v. d. Pers. Christi,* Abth. i p. 906 [*E. Tr.* Div. i vol. ii pp. 306—307]. That is to say *οὐσία* to him does not mean 'nature', but 'being' (*substantia*). The *οὐσία* of the Father is not like or similar to the *οὐσία* of the Son; it is one and the same. The *οὐσία* of both is GOD; the mode of existence, the condition, of one is described by the name Father; of the other by the name Son.

As regards Basil, accordingly, the evidence proves that he meant by *οὐσία* what Aristotle and Athanasius and every accurate writer and thinker before him had meant; that it is never to him the equivalent of φύσις, though φύσις will often express enough of the conception in his mind; and that again and again he expressly repudiates the notion that 'likeness' can describe the relation between the three hypostases of the one *οὐσία* of Godhead. Ὁμοούσιος certainly did not mean to him what ὁμοιούσιος meant to the Nicenes.

What οὐσία meant to Gregory of Nyssa.

To Gregory of Nyssa, the devoted younger brother of Basil, to whom he constantly refers as his 'master', *οὐσία* certainly did not mean 'nature', but what *substantia* meant to Tertullian. The whole argument and the careful distinction of terms which runs through many of his writings shews this. For instance, in the *De communibus notionibus* he insists that θεός is not a term (ὄνομα) προσώπων δηλωτικόν but οὐσίας σημαντικόν. It is one *οὐσία* and therefore it is one name that is used. With regard to the πρόσωπα you use the conjunction 'and'—saying Father and Son and Holy Spirit, because they are not the same but different πρόσωπα. But in regard to the term God usage is quite different (τῷ δὲ θεὸς ὀνόματι δηλωτικῷ τῆς οὐσίας ὄντι ἐκ *τινος ἰδιώματος προσόντος αὐτῆς οὐ συνάπτομεν τὸν καὶ σύνδεσμον, ὥστε λέγειν ἡμᾶς θεὸν καὶ θεὸν καὶ θεόν*). In this passage the *οὐσία* is incidentally distinguished from its *ἰδίωμα*, the character or nature belonging to it. And immediately afterwards the assertion that the Father is *οὐσία*, the Son *οὐσία*, and the Holy Spirit *οὐσία*, and yet that there are not three *οὐσίαι*, confirms beyond doubt the indication that by *οὐσία* is not meant nature. For it would be impossible to say the Father is nature, and the Son is nature, and the Holy Spirit nature. And again, when repeating that the name 'God' indicates *οὐσία*, he notes that it does not really present to us the *οὐσία* itself (for that is incomprehensible), but is taken from one of the *ἰδιώματα* which belong to the *οὐσία* and so designates it sufficiently if properly understood (Migne, vol. XLV p. 177). The name 'God' designates all through the *οὐσία*, and must therefore never be used in the plural.

The whole argument that follows (pp. 177, 180) with respect to an apparently different usage in regard to men, by which Peter, Paul, and Barnabas are styled "three men", is based on the same distinction, and would be unintelligible unless it were so based. It is only by a strange misunderstanding and perversion, which really makes nonsense of Gregory's careful logic, that *οὐσία* has been taken here as meaning nature. Gregory notes precisely the misleading character of popular usage, and declares that it is only *καταχρηστικῶς καὶ οὐ κυρίως* that we speak of 'many men', and that the use of the analogy between the divine *οὐσία* and the human *οὐσία* must be carefully guarded. Strictly and simply the name *ἄνθρωπος* signifies *οὐσία* as does the name *θεός*, and *quâ ἄνθρωπος* Peter and Paul and Barnabas are one. Each is only a particular *ὑπόστασις* of the one *οὐσία*[1].

The same reasoning runs through the Letter to Ablabius *Quod non sint tres Dii* (Migne, vol. XLV pp. 115—136). He speaks freely of *φύσις* and *τὸ κοινὸν τῆς φύσεως*, but says that

[1] The 'solidarity' of humanity could not be more certainly conceived than it is by Gregory. Humanity is essentially one, just as Deity is essentially one: there is one *οὐσία*—*ἄνθρωπος*, just as there is one *οὐσία*—*θεός*.

no title or attribute describes what the divine nature is κατ' οὐσίαν (p. 121)—what that which cannot suffer corruption *is* in itself.

And, seeking an illustration to shew that there are not many Gods, though there are three ὑποστάσεις, he chooses 'gold' and golden coins: the gold is one and the same, there are not many 'golds', though there are many golden coins (p. 132).

The unity of 'nature', which he speaks of most, is based upon the sameness of οὐσία.

The Scriptures, he argues, permit us to speak of men in the plural because no one would be led to imagine a plurality of 'manhoods', merely because the title of the nature was used in the plural. Τὸ δὲ θεὸς φωνὴν παρατετηρημένως κατὰ τὸν ἑνικὸν ἐξαγγέλλει τόπον, τοῦτο προμηθουμένη, τὸ μὴ διαφόρους φύσεις ἐπὶ τῆς θείας οὐσίας ἐν τῇ πληθυντικῇ σημασίᾳ τῶν θεῶν παρεισάγεσθαι... 'God' is always said in the singular διὰ τὸ μήτε φύσεως μήτε ἐνεργείας ἐνθεωρεῖσθαί τινα διαφορὰν τῇ θεότητι. The divine nature which is single and unchangeable rejects all ἑτερότης κατ' οὐσίαν—all ἑτερότης τῆς οὐσίας τῶν ὑποκειμένων (pp. 132, 133).

In like manner in the *Oratio Catechetica*, where he is most concerned to mark clearly the distinction of the ὑποστάσεις in the unity of the Godhead, he regularly speaks of the divine φύσις and of the human φύσις. But φύσις is not used as equivalent to οὐσία. The occasional use of οὐσία preserves the distinction. For instance, when he gives as one main difference between the divine φύσις and the human φύσις, that the former is unalterable while the latter is liable to change, it is clear that the οὐσία Man remains though the φύσις which is his may change and develope (ed. Krabinger § 21 "man was fashioned as an imitation of the divine nature, τρεπτῆς δὲ φύσεως ὢν κατ' ἀνάγκην"). So, while maintaining that the φύσις of the Godhead is always one and the same, he describes (§ 1) as its γνωρίσματα a number of qualities (such as goodness, power, wisdom, eternity, immortality, perfection)—that is to say the φύσις is identified with the qualities or attributes, but obviously that to which the φύσις belongs is the Godhead itself (viz. the οὐσία θεός). And again (§ 15) he concludes a reference to several attributes and capacities of man with the words οὔτε ἄλλο τι τοιοῦτον ὃ τῆς ἀνθρωπίνης ἴδιον οὐσίας ἐστί. And more particularly the phrases which he employs in his exposition of the doctrine of the Trinity prove the point, not less because he does not use the precise terms μία οὐσία and τρεῖς ὑποστάσεις conjoined. He says the Deity is distinguished τῇ ὑποστάσει and not divided in underlying essence (διακέκριται τῇ ὑποστάσει καὶ οὐ μεμέρισται τῷ ὑποκειμένῳ § 3). The three exist οὐσιωδῶς, each ἐν ἰδιαζούσῃ ὑποστάσει, each κατ' οὐσίαν τις ὑφεστῶσα δύναμις—a δύναμις οὐσιώδης: where no one would maintain that οὐσιώδης means 'natural' rather than 'substantial'. That τὸ ὑποκείμενον, the 'subject' matter, refers to the οὐσία, to which all qualities attach, is clear from the context, and from an analogy which is adduced (§ 16)—the analogy of birth and growth, in which in spite of all changes τὸ ὑποκείμενον remains the same[1].

And the same sense is found in his Answer to Eunomius' Second Book, in the discussion of the relation between οὐσία and τὸ ἀγέννητον.

What the terms meant to Gregory of Nazianzus.

Gregory of Nazianzus is entirely at one in this matter with his two Cappadocian brothers. His usage of the terms may be gathered distinctly from the third and the fifth of his *Theological Orations*. He, too, constantly uses φύσις where οὐσία *might* be used; just as we may speak without scientific precision of the divine nature without in any way intending to question the existence of the Godhead as a substantial entity, an οὐσία. We can constantly express by 'nature' all that we need to express. Similarly he too declares that, though attributes of God may be known, His οὐσία may not be known by man (iii 11); and he says that of the names revealed the one which simply declares the eternal substantive existence—ὁ ὤν—is the best (iv 18).

He argues (iii 2) that the *monarchia* is nevertheless a Triad, the oneness of which is constituted by φύσεως ὁμοτιμία, γνώμης σύμπνοια, and ταὐτότης κινήσεως—the unity being further guaranteed by the σύννευσις (consent, concord) with the One of those which are ἐξ αὐτοῦ, so that though there is a numerical

[1] A passage in ch. i (Krabinger, p. 8) in which he speaks of the relation between λόγος and νοῦς in us (the former proceeding from the latter, and neither being entirely the same nor yet altogether different—they are one κατὰ τὴν φύσιν but different τῷ ὑποκειμένῳ) reveals a usage of the terms apparently rather than really dissimilar. With it may be compared the reference of Basil to Dionysius Al. (*Ep.* ix 2), where τὸ ὑποκείμενον is used of that which distinguishes the Persons (οὐ ταυτὸν τῷ ὑποκειμένῳ of Father and Son). In these cases τὸ ὑποκείμενον is used rather in the third of the senses found in Aristotle: see Note on τὸ ὑποκείμενον p. 82.

difference there is no essential division or separation (*ὥστε κἂν ἀριθμῷ διαφέρῃ τῇ γε οὐσίᾳ μὴ τέμνεσθαι*). At this passage the latest editor draws attention to the fact that *οὐσία* means more than *φύσις* to Gregory[1].

So, too, the whole argument in regard to the Deity of the Holy Spirit (v 9 ff.) (though *φύσις* is sometimes used) depends on the conception of the *μία θεότης* (*εἷς θεός*) as a substantive entity —an *οὐσία* in the old sense—not simply *φύσις*; which substantive entity exists all through and in the three *ἰδιότητες* Father, Son, and Holy Spirit[2].

The cumulative weight of the evidence, accordingly, seems to be quite decisive against the suggestion that *ὁμοούσιος* meant to the Cappadocian Fathers only 'of one nature', so that it could be used in the case of the Godhead of three persons who were simply one in disposition and concord of will and certain common attributes.

If any doubt as to the usage of the Cappadocians remained, or if a single and decisive proof were required, the doubt would be resolved and the proof immediately furnished by reference to Gregory of Nyssa's statement of the doctrine which was afterwards known as the *περιχώρησις*. It had been expressed before by Dionysius of Rome (quoted by Ath. *de Decr.* 26) and Athanasius (esp. *Or. c. Ar.* iii 1–6), and in the *Makrostichos* § 9, and was more fully expounded by Augustine afterwards (*de Trin.* iv 30, viii *ad init.*). But Gregory makes the main point perfectly clear, and he does so with the express purpose and intention of repelling the notion that the relation between the Persons in the Godhead was really analogous to the relation of three men to

[1] The *Five Theological Orations of Gregory of Nazianzus*, Dr A. J. Mason, p. 75.

[2] *ὁμοούσιος* is frequently used and explained as meaning *μιᾶς οὐσίας* or *τῆς αὐτῆς οὐσίας*, e.g. v 11, 16, 19. Other passages illustrating the use are iii 13, *θεοῦ μίαν οὐσίαν καὶ φύσιν καὶ κλῆσιν* (so *οὐσία* is not equivalent to *φύσις*); iii 15, *τὸ ὑποκείμενον* takes the place of *οὐσία*; iii 16, *οὐσία* is distinguished from *σχέσις* and *τὸ πῶς ἔχει* ('substance' from relation); v 16, the sameness of the *οὐσία* and *δύναμις* is the ground of the closeness of the union and relation of the Three with one another; v 18, 19, some useful instances by way of illustration in answer to false reasoning from 'number'—things may be called three though different in *nature*, and yet may be named singly with a view to quantitative reality though conjoined in *οὐσία*—where the examples taken shew that *οὐσία* means more than *φύσις*. Cf. also the use of the verb *οὐσιοῦν*, ii 6, v 32; and the noun *οὐσίωσις*, iv 20; and the adj. *οὐσιώδης*, v 32 (the same sense being intended: see Mason, *ad loc.*).

their common humanity. He has said that the term 'Godhead' is really significant of ἐνέργεια—operation—rather than of nature, and then he goes on to mark the difference. The operations of men (even of those who are engaged in the same spheres of work) are separate and individual, whereas the operations of the Godhead are always effected by the Three together "without mark of time or distinction—"since there is no delay, existent or conceived, in the motion of the "divine will from the Father, through the Son, to the Spirit". "In "the case of the divine nature we do not learn that the Father does "any thing by himself in which the Son does not work conjointly, or "again that the Son has any special operation apart from the Holy "Spirit; but every operation which extends from God to the creation, "and is named according to our variable conceptions of it, has its "origin from the Father, and proceeds through the Son, and is per-"fected in the Holy Spirit." So "the unity existing in the action "prevents plural enumeration." (*Quod non sint tres Dii*, ad med.)

The thought is expressed in simple untechnical language, but the sense is that of careful definition. However the personal distinctions may be emphasized, no one of the Three is conceivable apart from the others: the full Godhead is in each one. That is to say, the One Godhead exists always as one substantial entity in three modes of being or spheres of action or mutual relations.

The significance of the absence of ἐκ τῆς οὐσίας from the Creed which prevailed.

Of the questions proposed there remains for us to determine the real significance of the absence of ἐκ τῆς οὐσίας from the Creed which took the place of the Nicene. What Dr Harnack says about it has been already quoted[1].

As to the import of the term itself Dr Zahn (p. 16 f.) notes that, before the acceptance of the ὁμοούσιον, the doctrine that the Son was begotten ἐκ τῆς οὐσίας τοῦ πατρός was established; and that it was only when it appeared that it was possible to elude the phrase ἐκ τῆς οὐσίας as well as the conception of the generation,

[1] pp. 7, 9, *supra*.

that ὁμοούσιον was seized upon as the final safeguard[1]. And he insists that by it was intended more than that the Father was the ground of the being of the Son—it was by no means only another expression for ἐκ τοῦ πατρός, as Eusebius tried to make the people of Caesarea believe[2]. It declares that the being which underlies the predicate 'Son' has its origin in the being of the Father; this latter continues in the former, and there are not two specimens of one species, but one divine being in two subjects. The subjects of Father and Son are a concrete unity: the phrase excludes the conception of them as a discrete plurality. So, I understand, Dr Zahn implies that when ἐκ τῆς οὐσίας is omitted, or indeed unless ἐκ τῆς οὐσίας is asserted in the Creed, we have a doctrine of the Godhead as a discrete plurality; that is, three individual beings in one *genus* or class together, instead of one Being existing in three 'subjects'[3].

The omission or the absence is undoubtedly a real *crux*: and in view of this fact Prof. Gwatkin (*Studies*, p. 262 note 1) in a tempting epigram exclaims "Surely Athanasius would have had "an anathema for the men who left out the all-important ἐκ τῆς "οὐσίας!" It might perhaps be permitted to doubt whether Athanasius was quite so ready with anathemas. But in any case we shall all be agreed that least of all men would *he* have contended for a *gloss* if once it was clear that the *sense* for which he had fought was at last accepted. And years before he had made it clear as day that he only valued this 'all-important' phrase because it prohibited the Arian interpretation of ἐκ θεοῦ.

In the phrase of the Creed ἐκ τῆς οὐσίας τοῦ πατρός there can be no doubt that οὐσία means the inmost being of the Father, his very self. The translation 'substance' which comes to us through the Latin is not satisfactory: 'essence' hardly conveys to English ears the real meaning: and 'nature'—though 'nature' is certainly included in the sense—is quite inadequate by itself. 'Being' is

[1] Inasmuch as Tertullian already has both *de substantia patris* and *unius substantiae*, Zahn's statement seems to need correction. v. Tert. *adv. Prax.* 4, 7, 8.

[2] Yet Athanasius (*de Decr.* 22, quoted *infra*) some five-and-twenty years after the Council gives just the same account of the intention of the phrase as Eusebius gave at the time.

[3] Cf. Dr Harnack's expressions cited *supra*, pp. 9, 10.

the nearest equivalent we have. The phrase is intended to mark the distinct personality of the Son on the one hand—he is in himself, he has his own existence; while on the other hand it declares that he has his existence from no source external to the Father[1], but is of the very being of the Father and belongs to his being—so that the Father himself is not, does not exist, is not to be conceived as having being, apart from the Son. On this point at any rate the gloss of Dr Zahn, already quoted, may be heartily accepted. So it is that Athanasius, writing in explanation of the proceedings at Nicaea[2], declares that the Council wrote 'from the *essence* of God'[3], rather than simply 'from God', expressly to mark the unique unoriginate relation in which the Son stands to the Father, in view of the sense in which it is true that all things are 'from God'. Of nothing originate could it be said that it was 'from the *essence* of God'. But the essence of the Father is the sphere of being of the Son. He is inseparable from the essence of the Father[4]. To say 'of the essence of God' is the same thing as to say 'of God' in more explicit language[5]. Here then we find Athanasius in set terms deliberately declaring that *ἐκ τῆς οὐσίας τοῦ θεοῦ* is merely an exegetical expansion of *ἐκ θεοῦ*, and insisting that the two phrases mean the same thing.

As soon as ever, therefore, it was clear that *ἐκ θεοῦ* would not be twisted from its natural sense, and that there was no danger of any Arian interpretation being put upon it, it is certain Athanasius would have gladly dropped the *ἐκ τῆς οὐσίας* which had become a

[1] The phrase is thus in emphatic contrast with the Arian *ἐξ οὐκ ὄντων*, by which they meant to express the origin of the Son external to the Father, but yet before there was anything else in existence. (Only God—the Father—existed in the beginning. Then the Son came into being. But as there was not anything existent but the Father, and it was not from the Father that the Son came into being, he must have derived his being from the non-existent.)

[2] *De Decretis* 19.

[3] This declaration of Athanasius that the Council wrote 'from the essence of God' (instead of 'of the Father'), and his interchange throughout this passage of the designations 'God' and 'the Father', is in itself not without significance. To the Christian conception of God both Father and Son are equally essential. As far as *οὐσία* goes, no distinction can be made between them. The *οὐσία* of the Son is the same as the *οὐσία* of the Father.

[4] *Ibid.* 20.

[5] *Ibid.* 22.

useless gloss. *Ὁμοούσιος* and *ἐκ θεοῦ* were then an ample safeguard of the truth. *Ἐκ τῆς οὐσίας* had proved an insuperable barrier against Arians through all their onslaughts on the faith. It had held the gate secure against them. But now that the Church no longer feared their attacks, the bar might be disused. *Ἐκ θεοῦ* was shibboleth enough.

So then, if the Church had ever deliberately, of set purpose, struck out the words from the Creed, the act would have had no doctrinal effect. She would still have continued to interpret *ἐκ θεοῦ* as *ἐκ τῆς οὐσίας τοῦ θεοῦ.* Or had she unconsciously ceased to use the words, without any formal act, she would still have intended their sense.

As a matter of fact, the explanation of the absence of the words from the Creed in common use is to be found in the curious history of that Creed. The Creed of Nicaea was never altered at all. It was almost certainly affirmed at Constantinople in 381 with *ἐκ τῆς οὐσίας* in it, and again, with a few interpolations, at Chalcedon in 451, in the same breath with the enlarged Jerusalem Creed which probably never contained the words at all[1]. The bishops assembled then had no conception that the doctrine of the Godhead and of the relation of the Son to the Father contained in the later Creed was not identical with the faith of the Nicene fathers, in which they had been baptized. The evidence surely shews conclusively that no support for such a conception could be drawn from the fact that *ἐκ τῆς οὐσίας* was not to be found in the later Creed[2].

Conclusion.

And so this examination may be brought to an end.

Dr Harnack noted (*supra* p. 4) that the acceptance of the term

[1] The words are in the current texts of Epiphanius, but Dr Hort does not regard them as belonging to the Creed. See the Creeds pp. 141, 143, 144 of Dr Hort's *Two Dissertations.*

[2] Dr Hort's comment on the revised Antiochian Creed is profoundly applicable here: "To regard either this or any other of the five known revised Creeds as lowerings of the Nicene standard for the sake of dogmatic compromise is to mistake their whole nature: the process in each case consisted in the enrichment of a local Symbol for local use." *Two Dissertations*, p. 128.

ὁμοούσιος in the sense of ὁμοιούσιος involved 'the most cruel satire'. Were the facts indeed as recent writers have represented them, the satire involved in them would be unbearable. Above all other men Athanasius deemed words to be mere counters, mere symbols of meaning: he only cared for the meaning itself, and again and again he urged the insignificance of terms in themselves; their value was only what they conveyed (cf. *ad Antiochenos*, 8). Any words—if only the sense which was intended was true. And he it is, of all men, who is given at last the words which were chosen at Nicaea—but in the sense against which he struggled all his life!

Such a conclusion would indeed be a scathing satire on the work of Councils and theologians[1]. More than fifty years of most distressing controversy, of cruel persecution, of weary exile and dejection, heart-burning and heart-breaking: Athanasius—the familiar noble figure 'against the world'—at last persuading some who were able after his death to carry on the struggle to apparent victory: the Nicene Faith at last triumphant—the whole Church of the East at last convinced that its terms alone express and safeguard so much of the truth as human minds can apprehend: the Nicene Creed again affirmed—its chief watchword proclaimed: and all in a different sense! the sense of that very rival term against which the whole battle had been waged, the term which did not furnish any safeguard against Arian conceptions, the indefinite term of futile compromise, which could satisfy neither Nicene nor Arian.

It is true, indeed, that proof that a Council, which only attained the honours of ecumenicity seventy years after it met, had erred, would cause the student of ecclesiastical history little surprise.

And incredible as it would be that the Church had all these centuries been committed to a semi-Arian interpretation of the Person of Christ; yet her practical faith in the reality of the Incarnation as being in very truth the union of GOD and Man

[1] It would, indeed, abundantly justify Gibbon's famous taunt that "the profane of every age have derided the furious contests which the difference of a single diphthong excited between the Homoousians and the Homoiousians."

might seem to have been so abundantly testified by fifteen centuries of fruitful life, that we might acquiesce in a conciliar blunder, full of thankfulness that it had been so over-ruled and robbed of power to hurt.

In the interests merely of traditional definitions of the Faith this study need not have been attempted.

But historical truth demands that every student in turn shall weigh for himself the evidence from which the historian has to draw his inductions. He must not accept without examination theories which seem to him to be at variance with the facts, even though they are championed by scholars of highest repute. And so, in regard to the subject of this investigation, he is entitled to ask for more evidence than has yet been produced to justify the use of such terms as the 'neo-Nicene party' and the 'new sense' of *ὁμοούσιος*, when by these terms it is meant that for the doctrine declared at the Council of Nicaea was substituted, and accepted at Constantinople and ever afterwards by the Church, another doctrine—a doctrine which declared the Son to be not 'of the same' but 'of like' *οὐσία* with the Father.

Additional Notes.

(1) *Substantia.*

'Substantia' as the verbal from *substo* means 'that by which anything subsists or exists, or the essence or underlying principle by which each *res* is what it is'. So Seneca[1] (*Ep.* 58 ante med.) contrasts things which have *substantia* with those which only have an imaginary existence, being fashioned by unreal thought (falsa cogitatio), e.g. Centaur, giants: which shews the meaning to be 'real existence'. And Quintilian vii 2. 5 says that before you can enquire about a man, who he is, you must have his *substantia* before you (i.e. his real existence, the fact that he *is*), so that you cannot make the subject of examination the question of his *being* (ut non possit quaeri *an sit*)—that is to say, *substantia* denotes real existence, as to the particular form or character of which enquiry may be made. And in like manner Quintilian *ib.* 3. 6 distinguishes as subjects of investigation *substantia* and *qualitas*. [In this way it comes about that the *substantia* of a thing is an easy periphrasis for the thing itself, and the term is applied to things inanimate and abstract—e.g. Quintilian *substantia rhetoricae*, Boethius *substantia numeri*; and many other examples of this usage are found.]

The secondary sense of the term—'property', 'patrimony', 'fortune' (in this sense it is even used with the meaning 'slaves'—see references in Du Cange), has been sufficiently referred to in the text in connexion with Tertullian's usage (see *supra* p. 21).

It is in its primary sense that the word was adopted for doctrinal purposes in connexion with the attempt to describe the Godhead.

It had to do duty for both *οὐσία* and *ὑπόστασις*, though by derivation the exact equivalent of the latter only, since *essentia*, the proper representative of *οὐσία*, was not admitted to a permanent place in the Latin language. Seneca *Ep.* 58. 6 apologises for using *essentia* and shields himself under Cicero's name (Cicero also used *indoloria* saying 'licet enim novis rebus nova nomina imponere'—Forcellini); and Quintilian ii 14. 1, 2 speaks of it and *entia* together with *oratoria* (to represent *ῥητορική*) as equally harsh translations, only defensible on the ground of the poverty of language resulting from the banishment of terms formed from the Greek.

Accordingly the Latin translator of Irenaeus renders *οὐσία* and

[1] The following references are given by Forcellini.

ὑπόστασις alike by *substantia*[1]. It represents οὐσία in the following passages: I i 2 (ii 2) ἀναλελύσθαι εἰς τὴν ὅλην οὐσίαν, I i 3 (ii 4) ἐντεῦθεν λέγουσι πρώτην ἀρχὴν ἐσχηκέναι τὴν οὐσίαν (*substantiam materiae*), I i 3 (ii 5) τὴν δὲ ἐνθύμησιν αὐτῆς σὺν τῷ πάθει...εἶναι μὲν πνευματικὴν οὐσίαν, I i 5 (iii 3) εἰς ἄπειρον ῥεούσης τῆς οὐσίας...ἀνελύθη ἂν εἰς τὴν οὐσίαν αὐτῆς (sc. having lost μορφή), I i 7 (iv 1) μορφῶσαι μόρφωσιν τὴν κατ' οὐσίαν μόνον ἀλλ' οὐ τὴν κατὰ γνῶσιν, *ibid.* σύστασιν καὶ οὐσίαν τῆς ὕλης γεγενῆσθαι...ἔνυγρον οὐσίαν [but below § 8 ἔνυδρος οὐσία is rendered *humida materia*], I i 8 (iv 5) πρὸς τὸ γενέσθαι δύο οὐσίας, τὴν φαύλην τῶν παθῶν, τήν τε τῆς ἐπιστροφῆς ἐμπαθῆ, I i 9 (v 1) διακρίναντα γὰρ τὰς δύο οὐσίας συγκεχυμένας, I i 10 (v 4) οὐκ ἀπὸ ταύτης δὲ τῆς ξηρᾶς γῆς, ἀλλ' ἀπὸ τῆς ἀοράτου οὐσίας. In all these cases οὐσία is the *substratum* of the thing or being—having of course particular qualities or form in each particular case, but conceived of as apart from its qualities or form.

It represents ὑπόστασις in the following passages: I i 1 ὀγδοάδα, ῥίζαν καὶ ὑπόστασιν τῶν πάντων, I i 10 (v 3) τὴν λοιπὴν πᾶσαν ψυχικὴν ὑπόστασιν, *ibid.* τὴν πνευματικὴν τῆς πονηρίας ὑπόστασιν, I i 11 (vi 2) τὴν πνευματικὴν ὑπόστασιν, V xiii 3 ὅτι θνητὴ καὶ φθαρτὴ οὖσα ἀθάνατος καὶ ἄφθαρτος γίνεται, οὐκ ἐξ ἰδίας ὑποστάσεως, ἀλλὰ κατὰ τὴν τοῦ Κυρίου ἐνέργειαν (of the transformation of the flesh—Lat. 'non secundum propriam substantiam sed secundum Domini operationem'): in all which instances ὑπόστασις expresses almost exactly what οὐσία expresses in the cases preceding: and in the following passages, in which ὑπόστασις cannot be said to add any fresh conception to the noun with which it is joined, but the phrase is in effect a mere periphrasis such as is noted above in regard to the usage of *substantia* in Latin—V i 1 οὐ γὰρ δοκήσει ταῦτα, ἀλλ' ἐν ὑποστάσει ἀληθείας ἐγένετο (= in very truth), V ii 2 (ii 3) ἡ τῆς σαρκὸς ἡμῶν ὑπόστασις (= ἡ σὰρξ ἡμῶν), V v 1 καὶ Ἠλίας, ὡς ἦν ἐν τῇ τοῦ πλάσματος ὑποστάσει, ἀνελήφθη (in his created body, i.e. in his real body), V xii 3 τί οὖν ἦν τὸ ἀποθνῆσκον; πάντως ἡ τῆς σαρκὸς ὑπόστασις (= ἡ σάρξ).

In other passages in which *substantia* occurs we have only the

[1] Mr F. C. Burkitt has pointed out to me that, whether the Latin translation of Irenaeus was made in the second century or in the fourth century, there is no doubt that *substantia* was the second century equivalent of οὐσία. The rendering of οὐσία by *substantia* is at least as old as the earliest Latin version of the Gospels; for in Mk. ix 49 *k* has *omnia autem substantia consumitur*, a mistranslation of πᾶσα δὲ (or γὰρ) οὐσία ἀναλωθήσεται as conjectured by Dr Hort (*Intr.* p. 101). The conjecture is supported by θυσία (sic) ἀναλωθήσεται in Ψ.

Latin and cannot say with certainty whether it represents οὐσία or ὑπόστασις.

Tertullian in his use of the term ranges over all its possible meanings. In the sense of possessions or property he has it *Apol.* 39 of Christians who 'ex substantia familiari fratres sumus', *de exhort. cast.* 10 'magnam substantiam sanctitatis', *adv. Marc.* iv 15 'vir ob substantiam honorabilis'. He has it also in cases where it is little more than a periphrastic form of expression for the noun with which it is joined—*de cult. fem.* ii 2 'tota fidei substantia' (= tota fide), *adv. Prax.* 25 'tota substantia quaestionis istius' (the whole [matter] of that enquiry)[1]; and in cases in which it is defined as a particular manner of existence—*Apol.* 48 'superinduti substantia propria aeternitatis', *ad martyr.* 3 'brabium angelicae substantiae' (i.e. the prize of martyrdom is the angelic life—existence as angels).

But the regular philosophical sense on which the doctrinal use of the term is really based—the sense it has in the passages referred to in the account given above (pp. 16 f.)—is also the sense in, for example, *de anima* 11, where he distinguishes between the soul as *substantia* and its acts or operations (e.g. it is *spiritus, non proprie* but *quia spirat*). The same sense holds in the various adjectival forms which he employs. E.g. *de res. carn.* 45, in discussing the relation between the 'old man' and the 'new man', he argues that the difference is *moral* not *substantial* (*substantialis*)—that is to say, the *substantia* man is the same. Cf. the adverb *substantialiter*, *adv. Marc.* iv 35. So *adv. Valent.* 27 he refers to the idea that the animal and fleshly Christ suffered after the pattern of the higher Christ who for the making of Achamoth *substantivali non agnitionali forma* had leant upon a cross (i.e. Horus). And he uses *substantivus* (οὐσιώδης) in the same way—e.g. *adv. Prax.* 7 he comments on the Monarchian wish to avoid the recognition of the Son as a distinct entity (substantivus—a *res* or *persona*) and *ib.* 26 declares he is a *substantiva res*, whereas 'virtus altissimi' and the like are not, but only *accidentia substantiae* (just as *adv. Hermog.* 36 a *substantiva res* is contrasted with *accidens substantiae et corpori*). So too *adv. Hermog.* he mentions the heretics who wanted to make out that the 'beginning' ('ipsum principium in quo Deus fecit et caelum et terram') was something 'quasi substantivum et corpulentum quod in materiam interpretari possit'; and *de res. carn.* 40 maintains that *fides* and *dilectio* are not

[1] Cf. *de Orat.* 4 in the petition "Thy will be done" the prayer is made 'substantiam et facultatem voluntatis suae subministret nobis'.

'substantiva animae', but 'conceptiva' (that is not the *substantia* but the concepts of the *substantia*).

This difference which Tertullian defines (in accordance with the established use of the terms) between *substantia* and the nature of *substantia* practically held its ground throughout the later movements of Latin theology. *Substantia* is the term regularly employed to express the being of God—the Godhead in itself, as a distinct entity. The *substantia* has its own *natura* which is inseparable from it, but it is not its nature. The distinction does not seem to have been blurred in Latin as the distinctions between *οὐσία* and *φύσις* and *ὑπόστασις* and *πρόσωπον* were sometimes in Greek[1]. *Natura* does not appear to be used as *φύσις* was for example by Apollinarius and to some extent by Cyril (e.g. in his Anathemas against Nestorius the distinction between *ὑπόστασις* and *φύσις* is uncertain). Marius renders the *ὑπόστασις* of Cyril sometimes by *substantia*, sometimes by *subsistentia*; while Cyril's use of *φύσις*, understood by Nestorius in its proper sense, was obviously so unguarded and lacking in precision that it was at times equivalent to *ὑπόστασις* or 'person'.

The retention of the distinction is most plainly perceived in the expression of the doctrine of the Person of Christ—the union of the Godhead and the Manhood. Latin theologians hesitate to speak of the union of the two 'natures' merely. If they do not employ the term *substantia*, speaking of the *substantia* of Godhead and the *substantia* of manhood as united in the Person of the Son, they use some other phrase to represent it rather than *natura*. For example *forma Dei* and *forma servi* are preferred by Hilary, and also *filius Dei* and *filius hominis* by Augustine (as by Novatian long before); and Leo, though he freely uses *utraque natura*, is careful to mark his full meaning by adding 'et substantia' to *natura*, and by interchanging with it the expression *utraque* forma—*forma* conveying a more definite conception of an actual entity (a substantial existence) than *natura*.

Hilary's peculiar presentation of the doctrine of the *κένωσις* (whether it was entirely consistent with conciliar definitions of the doctrine of the Person of Christ or not, does not concern us at the moment) brings into strong relief his usage of the terms *forma Dei* and *forma servi* and *natura*. The Logos, he argues, must take the servant's form into himself, to effect a real union between the divine and the

[1] Origen kept the distinction between *οὐσία* and *φύσις*, and regularly spoke of the *οὐσία and* the *φύσις* of the Godhead—see e.g. the passages cited *infra* p. 77. Augustine's *obiter dictum de Trin.* vii 11 is an obvious error.

human and to elevate humanity: but the *forma Dei* and the *forma servi* cannot co-exist in one person at the same time. The Logos however remains himself all through and therefore cannot empty himself of his nature—the *divina natura* remains the same throughout and that he cannot resign. The *exinanitio* or *evacuatio* cannot go so far as to abolish the identity of the person. He who exists in the *forma servi* is no other than he who exists in the *forma Dei*. So the *exinanitio*, which makes the assumption of the *forma servi* possible, is really a continuous process by which he is always foregoing the use of the *forma Dei*, which is the expression of the divine nature—the divine nature, nevertheless, always belonging to him with all its attributes, and operating to the benefit of mankind. For the phrase *forma Dei* he elsewhere has *substantia*, and says the *substantia quae assumta habebatur* existed, but no longer that *quae in aliud se evacuando concesserat*. Hilary's expression of his thought is not quite free from ambiguity, but it is clear that he distinguishes between the subject Godhead and its nature; and so far he carries on the ancient Latin tradition. (See esp. *de Trin.* 9. 14, 11. 18, 10. 50 and Dorner *Doctrine of the Person of Christ*, E. Tr. I ii p. 405 ff.)

And Vincent of Lerinum shews the permanence of the Latin tradition in his account of the controversies which Leo had in view. The clearness of Latin usage enabled Vincent to put the case without the ambiguities with which it was confused for Greeks. He describes (*Common.* xii, xiii, ed. Hurter §§ 34—37) the error of Apollinarius as the refusal to recognise in Christ two substances—*duas substantias*—the one divine and the other human; whereas Nestorius, pretending to discriminate the two *substances* in Christ, really introduces two *persons*: and he sets out as the Catholic faith 'in God one substance, but three persons; in Christ two substances, but one person'. So he can say: "In God one substance but three persons....The *person* of Father is "one, of Son another, of Holy Spirit another; but yet the *nature* of "the Father and of the Son and of the Holy Spirit is not other and "other, but one and the same" (§ 37); and again, in declaring that Jesus Christ is true man, not pretended, he insists that it was not the *person* of a man that he assumed, but that while his own *substance* remained unchangeable, he took upon (*or* into) himself the *nature* of perfect man (§ 39). Using *substantia* throughout—defined either by *divina* (or *divinitatis*) or *humana* (or *humanitatis*)—and retaining Tertullian's distinction, he can also speak with perfect lucidity of the '*natura* substantiae'.

So too in the Chalcedonian definition of the doctrine, in terms entirely consonant with the teaching and discrimination of Latin theologians from Tertullian to Leo, first, there is recognised in the person of Jesus Christ the two *substantiae* of Godhead and manhood (He is *unius substantiae* with the Father, *secundum deitatem*, and also *unius substantiae* with us, *secundum humanitatem*), and then it is declared that the one person exists in the two *natures*.

(2) *Persona*, *πρόσωπον*.

In regard to the Latin word *persona* the most important fact to notice is that, during the period with which we have to deal, it practically never means what 'person' means in modern popular usage. The sense of *persona* is different, even when it seems to be used very nearly in the sense of 'person', and when through the poverty of language it has no other representative in English as adequate as 'person'. It is always—even in such cases—a person looked at from some distinctive point of view, a person in particular circumstances; and the word conveys the notion much more of the environment than of the subject.

The history outside ecclesiastical use is clear.

It is first an actor's mask; and then by an easy transition the part the actor plays, which is represented by his mask; and so any part or rôle assumed by anyone without regard to its duration.

It is secondly the *condicio, status, munus* which anyone has among men in general, and in particular in civil life. And so it is the man himself so far as he has this or that *persona*. Thus slaves, as not possessing any rights of citizenship, were regarded by Roman law as not having *persona*: they were *ἀπρόσωποι* or *persona carentes*[1].

From this second sense of *persona*, then, ecclesiastical usage starts.

In the Latin translation of Irenaeus it occurs, I believe, once only (III xi 12 = xi 9) representing *πρόσωπον*, in a passage in which, having spoken of the fourfold character of the Gospels and supported it by illustrations (the four quarters of the world, the four winds, the image of the four beasts Apoc. iv 7, the four covenants given to men), Irenaeus goes on to censure the ignorance and folly of the heretics who

[1] E.g. 'Servi personam legibus non habent' (Senator *lib.* 6 *Ep.* 8 quoted by Du Cange), and the phrase *personam amittere*, where *persona* means rights, legal status, or position. It is this general sense of *condicio, status, munus* that is still seen in the Vulgate rendering of *πρόσωπον λαμβάνειν*—viz. *respicere* or *aspicere personam*, e.g. Mt. xxii 16, Lk. xx 21, Ecclesiasticus xxxv (xxxii) 16.

corrupt the Gospels, disregarding the idea (? plan) of the Gospel and mischievously introducing more or fewer πρόσωπα than the four (ἀθετοῦντες τὴν ἰδέαν τοῦ εὐαγγελίου, καὶ εἴτε πλείονα εἴτε ἐλάττονα τῶν εἰρημένων παρεισφέροντες εὐαγγελίων πρόσωπα). Here it means apparently 'forms', 'parts' as it were in the great drama of the Gospel history, which was destined (as Irenaeus argues) to be set forth to the world in the four familiar aspects.

Tertullian has the word in its primary sense of the actor's mask or rôle; e.g. *de carne Christi* 11 'nemo ostendere volens hominem, cassidem aut personam ei inducit'; and *de spectac.* 23 'ipsum opus personarum, quaero, an deo placeat, qui omnem similitudinem vetat fieri, quanto magis imaginis suae': and in the special sense in the phrase which represents πρόσωπον λαμβάνειν 'shew partiality'; e.g. *Apol.* 36, Christians must be friends not only to emperors—to the government, the state—but to all men, for 'nullum bonum sub exceptione personarum administramus', where the word certainly does not mean individuals but particular kinds of men, 'classes' perhaps; and *de pudicit.* 5 where he asserts that it is *personae acceptatio* to distinguish as to sin between idolatry and homicide on the one hand and adultery on the other.

But in general the word is used by Tertullian to designate *status*, or character, or part, or function: not of course that it is conceived as separate from some living subject or agent, but that attention is fixed on the character or function rather than on the subject or agent.

The following instances shew the usage plainly: *de monogam.* 7, after giving instances from the Old Testament with regard to monogamy, he says 'post vetera exempla originalium personarum' (i.e. after old instances of primitive 'characters'); *de paenit.* 11, of candidates for office, 'ad omnem occursum maioris cuiusque personae decrescentes' (i.e. anyone of higher status); *adv. Marc.* iv 14 he argues that the text Lk. vi 22 shews that Christ has come, for the hatred of the name of Christian could not have preceded the *personam nominis* (that is, the bearer of the name, the one whose part it was); and so even *de cor.* 1 'murmur tribuno defertur, et persona iam ex ordine accesserat' (not 'some one' or 'the man', but rather one occupying the position and playing the part already described, the *dei miles*—'the actor', the 'persona dramatis' of later phrase).

So too he uses the adjective *personalis* in a corresponding sense. E.g. *de res. carn.* 21 he argues against the *allegorical* interpretation of predictions as to the resurrection on the ground that in respect of other things the plain and *literal* sense of prophecy is generally recognised—in regard to cities and nations and kings the decrees and judgments of God which deal with seasons and places and characters are clearly shewn in prophecy ('temporalia et localia et personalia dei decreta atque iudicia in urbes et gentes et reges'). And again, in one of the few cases in which the word is closely connected with the expression of the doctrine of the Godhead, *adv. Prax.* 15, he says there is a visible and an invisible God. Scripture proves it. "I find both in the "Gospels and in the Epistles a visible and an invisible God, with the "recognition of a clear functional distinction in the condition of "each, i.e. the mode of existence or 'status' of each ('sub manifesta et "personali distinctione condicionis utriusque')." And in like manner the adverb *personaliter* is contrasted with *substantialiter* in his description of the Valentinian conception of God: *adv. Valent.* 7 'hunc substantialiter quidem αἰῶνα τέλειον appellant, personaliter vero προαρχὴν et τὴν ἀρχήν...', i.e. regarded as to his very being in itself—his 'substantia'—he has one designation; but regarded as to a particular mode of existence in his manifestation and functions he is otherwise described (cf. God as to *substantia*, Father as to *persona*).

It is to Tertullian's usage of the term *persona*, closely allied as it was with general Latin use, that we must look for its meaning in the later ecclesiastical definitions. It is clear that *persona* means in a single word precisely what Basil's τρόπος ὑπάρξεως expressed, and what ὑπόστασις was ultimately narrowed down to mean. Here again, then, we find that Latin theology, by its clearness and simplicity of terms, led the way to accurate description.

Though the history of πρόσωπον is somewhat similar, as to its primary uses, to that of *persona*[1], it is probably as a translation of the

[1] In the N.T. the regular sense of the word is 'face': either literally (of living beings or *trop.* of the face of the earth, e.g. Lk. xxi 35, Acts xvii 26), or as equivalent to 'presence'. In this sense the word occurs frequently throughout the N.T. It is also found in the special phrase πρόσωπον λαμβάνειν and cognate expressions, which have been referred to above. Usages peculiar to St Paul are (1) the contrast between πρόσωπον and καρδία, the outward and the inward, e.g. 1 Thess. ii 17 (where πρόσωπον means nearly 'presence') and 2 Cor. v 12 (where it denotes 'outward show' or 'demeanour' as contrasted with real feeling); (2) the phrase ἐν προσώπῳ Χριστοῦ 2 Cor. ii 10, iv 6 (the usage nearest to Tertullian's use of 'persona' for 'character' or 'part') = 'on the part of' or 'as representing' Christ, and 'in the rôle of'—'in the part played by'—almost 'in the person of' Christ, so later ἐκ προσώπου 'in the name of'; and (3) closely allied to (2), in 2 Cor. i 11, almost exactly like Tertullian's use of *persona*.

It is possible that Tertullian was fortified in his adoption of the word by the old

Latin term that it is first found in connexion with Christian doctrine[1]. There seems to be no reason in the nature of things why it should not have served Greek theology as *persona* ultimately served the Latins. But it was entirely spoiled for doctrinal purposes by the use which Sabellius and his followers made of it and its derivatives. When

Latin version of these passages. In the *adv. Hermog.* 18 he quotes Prov. viii 30 *quotidie autem oblectabar in persona eius* (cf. *adv. Prax.* 6), which closely represents the LXX version ἐν προσώπῳ αὐτοῦ. He may be simply translating as he writes, for there appears to be no other O. L. evidence for *persona* here: but in any case the word must either have the primary meaning 'face', or be a periphrasis for the person himself (=ἐν αὐτῷ).

[1] The word is first found in connexion with Christian doctrine in Hippolytus *contra Noetum* § 7 τὸ γάρ ἐσμεν οὐκ ἐφ' ἑνὸς λέγεται, ἀλλ' ἐπὶ δύο πρόσωπα ἔδειξεν, δύναμιν δὲ μίαν and § 14 δύο μὲν οὐκ ἐρῶ θεοὺς ἀλλ' ἢ ἕνα, πρόσωπα δὲ δύο (cf. *Ref. Haer.* ix 12). That is to say, the Greek term first appears in the writing of a Roman theologian, who won a considerable reputation in the East.

The assertion that Hippolytus, though he writes in Greek, thinks in Latin, and that his style is steeped in Latin idioms (C. Bigg, *Christian Platonists* p. 165), is perhaps exaggerated. But there can be little doubt that we must look to Rome itself for the place where he learnt his theology (although he was certainly indebted to Irenaeus for teaching, by lecture first and afterwards by his published works). Accordingly we may take him as representing Western usage; cf. Lightfoot, *S. Clement of Rome* vol. ii p. 422 'We...look to Rome itself, or at all events not further than the South of Gaul, for the place of his Christian schooling'. It is therefore probable that the term *persona* was already familiar at Rome, and that πρόσωπον here is a translation of it. Hippolytus is not likely to have derived it from Irenaeus (see *supra* p. 70). That it came to him from Tertullian directly is hardly probable. He does not shew the precision of terminology which would be expected from a reader of Tertullian. Though he has πρόσωπον (=persona) he does not use the equivalent of *substantia* in connexion with the doctrine of the Godhead. (He has μονοούσια of things created, meaning composed entirely of one element or ἀρχή, *Ref. Haer.* x 32 *ad init.*; and he repudiates the notion that the humanity of the incarnate Logos is of a different οὐσία from ours *ib.* x 33: but he has nothing like Tertullian's *una substantia in tribus cohaerentibus.*) But while our knowledge of the chronology of the lives of Hippolytus and Tertullian is so meagre, the relations between them cannot be certainly determined.

[The relation between Noetus and Praxeas, and more particularly between the *contra Noetum* of Hippolytus and the *adversus Praxean* of Tertullian, calls for further investigation. Noeldechen (*Jahrb. f. Prot. Theol.* vol. xiv 1888) maintains that the African writer was indebted to the Roman (Lightfoot, *S. Clement of Rome* vol. ii p. 418, incidentally accepts this view), and goes so far as to style Tertullian's treatise 'only an echo' of the earlier work of Hippolytus. This seems to me an extraordinary judgment, indeed a paradox, alike on literary and on dogmatic grounds. There are of course resemblances between the two writings, for both are dealing with the same subject; but the general impression which the two treatises it had once been definitely employed to express the conception of distinctions in the Godhead which were merely temporary and external, different parts played in the process of self-revelation to the world and to men by one and the same Person, it was almost impossible that it should ever be adopted to denote distinctions which were eternal and rooted in the very being of the Godhead, entirely apart from any relation to the created universe and the human race.

Like the Latin *persona* it was just the word that was wanted to express the thought of the three relations in which the one God always exists, the three distinct spheres of being—each representing special functions—which together make up the divine life. There was no reason why it should not have connoted all the notion of permanent 'personality' which properly attaches to the names of Father, Son, and Holy Spirit. It could easily have been safeguarded in use from limitation to merely temporary rôles (or parts or characters or functions) assumed simply for particular purposes. But Sabellius stole the word away; and Greek theologians were left without any suitable way of expressing the conception, till they could agree among themselves to use another term which properly meant something quite different, and could win general acceptance for the artificial sense which they put upon the term they used.

(3) *οὐσία—ὑπόστασις.*

The research of many scholars, from the days of Athanasius to those of Suicer and Bull and their successors, has made it easy to give the usage of the two terms *οὐσία* and *ὑπόστασις.*

produce suggests the independent work of two very different minds; and Tertullian's seems to me to be by far the more penetrating and comprehensive, the stronger and abler. A single example of the supposed indebtedness of Tertullian to Hippolytus may be taken pending a closer examination of the whole question. Noeldechen lays stress on the fact that rather more than half of the direct scriptural quotations of Hippolytus are 'found again' in Tertullian. An investigation of this fact leads to the following results. Tertullian cites very many more passages than does Hippolytus. As regards those which they have in common: (1) the grouping and collocation of the passages is not the same; (2) some of the passages are handled by the two writers quite differently and are introduced for different purposes; (3) some are the 'texts' on which the Monarchians are expressly said to have based their teaching, and therefore every writer on the subject would be bound to deal with them; (4) the others are the most obvious texts which would occur to anyone.]

The former (οὐσία) was first in the field, and has upon it the stamp of Plato himself. It was the characteristic of the Ideas, which are prior to all things that we know and see—the Ideas by imitation of which, or participation in which, things are what they are. The Ideas are the realities (τὰ ὄντα) as contrasted with the appearances on earth (τὰ φαινόμενα). So οὐσία is real existence, actual being—that which actually is; and each class of things has its own particular οὐσία, namely the Idea (so far, that is to say, as anything but the Idea can be regarded as existent at all).

It was, however, Aristotle who fixed for later times the usage of the word. To him it is (besides being commonly used to express 'possessions', 'property'—as *substantia* in Latin) equivalent to τὸ εἶναι: but particularly he uses it in closely allied senses expressive of real concrete existence—τὸ ὄν, τὸ ἁπλῶς ὄν. It is the first in the series of categories, 'substance': to it attach and from it are distinguished all conceptions of quantity or quality, all συμβεβηκότα. And thus, in accordance with Aristotle's inductive method, by a reverse process compared with that of Plato, it is primarily and properly descriptive of individual particular existence—each particular entity—the τόδε τι: and this primary sense is distinguished as πρώτη οὐσία. But inasmuch as there may be many examples of one particular οὐσία, it may signify that which is common to them all—to whole species or classes; and this secondary sense of the word is distinguished as δευτέρα οὐσία. Furthermore, inasmuch as every perceptible substance is conceived as consisting of matter and form, so οὐσία may be used of the whole entity, or of the material, or of the formal element: and it is often joined and combined with the term specially appropriated to either one or the other. In like manner it is found side by side with φύσις too (as well as with εἶδος). And not uncommonly it is used by itself where for the immediate purposes it seems that the sense required might be conveyed by φύσις. But in none of these cases does Aristotle ever employ it as a mere synonym for φύσις. It always means much more: including φύσις perhaps, but logically to be discriminated from it[1].

Ὑπόστασις, as a philosophical term, is a later and much rarer word[2]; but it is derived directly and naturally from an earlier and not

[1] For the usage of Aristotle see the careful arrangement in Bonitz's Index vol. v of Bekker's Edition, and the passages cited by Ritter and Preller.

[2] It is frequently used by Aristotle in its literal meaning 'a standing beneath' or 'that which stands beneath',—so either of the action of subsiding or of that which remains as a result of such action, viz. 'sediment':—but only one instance

uncommon use of the verb of which it is the noun. The *οὐσία* was said to exist at the outset, to be the underlying existence (*ὑφεστάναι*); and so the noun *ὑπόστασις* was a possible equivalent for *οὐσία* expressing the essential *substratum*, 'the vehicle of all qualities' (cf. *τὸ ὑποκείμενον*). The earliest examples of its use are found in Stoic writers, and thenceforward both words were current without any clear distinction being drawn between them; but *οὐσία* was by far the commoner term, *ὑπόστασις* being comparatively rarely found. So Socrates the historian could say (*H. E.* iii 7) 'the ancient philosophical writers scarcely noticed this word', though 'the more modern ones have frequently used it instead of *οὐσία*'. It was, however, as has been stated *supra* p. 65, the equivalent of *ὑπόστασις* (viz. *substantia*) which was acclimatized in the Latin language more readily than the equivalent of *οὐσία* (viz. *essentia*), and therefore *substantia* was all through the normal term by which Latin theologians expressed the conceptions for which *οὐσία* stood.

The author of the Epistle to the Hebrews (i 3) is the first writer who introduces the term into Christian theology. In his phrase *χαρακτὴρ τῆς ὑποστάσεως αὐτοῦ*, *ὑπόστασις* is exactly the equivalent of *οὐσία* ('being', 'essence', 'substance', as in the *μία οὐσία*, *una substantia*, of later technical theology), as it was expounded by the later Greek theologians, who would themselves have used *οὐσία* there instead and have kept *ὑπόστασις* to express the characteristics of the existence of the 'Persons' of the Trinity.

By Tatian it is regularly used instead of *οὐσία* (he does not use the term *οὐσία* at all) to express: (1) the *substratum*, the underlying principle or essence, that gives reality to a thing and constitutes it what it is, *Oratio* § 5: (2) a particular existence, a substantial entity, *ib.* § 21, of the gods of the old mythologies *φύσεως ὑποστάσεις* (? natural

of its use by him in a metaphysical sense is quoted, *Met.* 4. 395ᵃ 30, where (in regard to phantasms in the air) the phrase *καθ' ὑπόστασιν* (in contrast to *κατ' ἔμφασιν*) is equivalent to *κατ' ἐνέργειαν* or *τῷ ὄντι*. The derived sense 'foundation' or 'ground of support' *perhaps* appears in the region of ethics as *firmness* or *confidence*, e.g. Heb. iii 14; 2 Cor. ix 4, xi 17, though the later metaphysical conception is at least possible in all these instances (cf. the Vulgate and Tyndale's versions), at least the meaning 'subject-matter', 'the matter of'—for the thing itself (as *substantia* too was used). Dr Hatch (*Essays in Biblical Greek* pp. 88, 89) cites passages from the O.T. (Ruth i 12, Ps. xxxviii (xxxix) 8, Ezek. xix 5) to shew that the LXX translators used the word in the sense of confidence or hope: but he renders it in all cases '*ground* of hope' and sees in the word the significance of 'ground' or 'foundation' of anything.

objects, or hypostatisations of nature) καὶ στοιχείων διακοσμήσεις, *ib.* § 18, τῆς αὐτῆς ὑποστάσεώς ἐστιν (belong to the same *substantia*, sc. are ὑλικά): (3) a periphrasis for the thing itself of which it is said, e.g. § 6 ἐν ὑποστάσει τῆς σαρκικῆς ὕλης, § 21 σέβειν δὲ τῶν στοιχείων τὴν ὑπόστασιν οὔτ' ἂν πεισθείην, § 15 ἡ τῶν δαιμόνων ὑπόστασις.

Athenagoras has the word once in immediate connexion with οὐσία (*Leg.* 24 ἡ τῆς οὐσίας ὑπόστασις = ἡ οὐσία) in a quite general sense, while he uses οὐσία commonly in its stead—but only once of God (the 'being' of God, *de Res.* 1).

The author of the Epistle to Diognetus bids him consider of what ὑπόστασις are those whom he deems to be gods (viz. of stone and brass and wood and silver and the like) § 2.

The regular use of such technical terms by theologians was doubtless greatly stimulated by the Gnostics (cf. Irenaeus I v 1), and Irenaeus in writing against them constantly uses both ὑπόστασις and οὐσία without distinction: see e.g. the passages cited in the Note on *Substantia* (p. 66).

The first to attempt a scientific discrimination between οὐσία and ὑπόστασις was Origen; but he did it with a very uncertain hand[1].

Thus, he uses οὐσία regularly to express existence, being, 'essence', exactly as Tertullian uses *substantia*, in reference to the Godhead of the Trinity[2]. But he can also use the same word where he wishes to express the 'personal' existence which belongs to the Son as distinct from the Father[3]. But the sense of need of a more

[1] See C. Bigg: *Christian Platonists of Alexandria* pp. 163 ff.—from whose references the following passages are selected.

[2] E.g. *in Joh. Tom.* x 21 he speaks of some who draw from sayings of Christ the wrong inference 'that the Son does not differ from the Father numerically, but that Father and Son are both one, οὐ μόνον οὐσίᾳ ἀλλὰ καὶ ὑποκειμένῳ, and are said to be different according to their particular predicates (κατά τινας ἐπινοίας), not κατὰ ὑπόστασιν; *de orat.* 23 the phrase 'Our Father *which art in heaven*' is used to separate as it were the οὐσία of God from all things that have come into being; and *in Num.* Hom. xii 1, *in Rom.* vii 13, viii 5 (in which three passages the Greek is no longer extant, but οὐσία was probably the original of the Latin translation 'substantia') where it is declared that the *natura* and *substantia* of the Trinity—Father, Son, and Holy Spirit—are one and the same. (In *de princip.* i 25 *Latin*—a quotation of Heb. i 3—*substantia* represents ὑπόστασις.)

[3] E.g. *de orat.* 15 the Son is ἕτερος τοῦ πατρὸς κατ' οὐσίαν καὶ ὑποκείμενον; *in Joh. Tom.* ii 18 *ad init.*—a reference to the fear lest the fact that the Saviour and God (the Father) are both called 'Light' should imply that the Father and the Son do not differ τῇ οὐσίᾳ; and *ib.* i 30 the predicates that apply to the Saviour may be separated (sc. logically) without infringing the unity of his οὐσία.

precise terminology is shewn by the efforts at closer definition which are made, and the qualifications which narrow down its meaning.

Thus, while the term *ὑπόστασις* is used for 'person', e.g. *in Joh.* ii 6, *τρεῖς ὑποστάσεις πειθόμενοι τυγχάνειν*, we find also in the same passage *οὐσία ἰδία*, and in the near context (*in Joh.* ii 2) *ἰδιότης* and *οὐσία κατὰ περιγραφήν* (i.e. *οὐσία* with a limitation—in a limited sense[1]).

It cannot therefore be maintained that the term *ὑπόστασις* received from Origen the value which was attached to it at the end of the following century. Its use as the equivalent of *οὐσία* was too firmly rooted. Nor does the evidence to be adduced from the correspondence of the Dionysii support the view that already by that time the limited sense of *ὑπόστασις* was established at Alexandria. The supposition that it was so—that the *τρεῖς ὑποστάσεις* of Dionysius of Alexandria meant to him exactly what the same phrase meant to the Cappadocian Fathers—is of course extremely tempting; but the temptation to antedate in this way the development of precision of terminology in this connexion must be resisted. Reasons have already been given in the text which seem to prohibit this interpretation. The fragments of the correspondence which are extant shew that Dionysius had not gained the conception of such a clear distinction. He realised three forms of existence much more vividly than one substantial entity of Deity. If the discrimination had been in any way due to him, it is impossible—so great was his reputation—that it could have died out in the great theological school of his see; and the whole history of the subsequent century proves conclusively that no more at Alexandria than anywhere else in the East had the implied precision of terms been attained.

So the framers of the Creed of Nicaea and its anathemas still used *οὐσία* and *ὑπόστασις* as synonyms[2], and as synonyms still the Arianizing parties in the Church in subsequent years put both words alike under the ban.

Thus it is that Athanasius *de Decr.* 20, repeating the anathema to the Nicene Creed, has only *ἐξ ἑτέρας οὐσίας*, shewing that to him at least no new conception was added by the alternative *ὑποστάσεως*; and in one of his latest writings *ad Afros* 4, refuting the objections brought against them as non-scriptural, he uses the terms as synonymous: "*ὑπόστασις* is *οὐσία* and means nothing else but simply being: which

[1] In the two passages cited *supra in Joh.* x 21 and *de orat.* 15 *ὑποκείμενον* is used in the narrower sense of the *substratum* of individual existence: elsewhere, e.g. *in Jerem.* Hom. viii 2, it is simply the 'subject'.

[2] *ὑπόστασις* (=*substantia*) was probably intended for the West.

"Jeremiah calls existence (ὕπαρξις).... For ὑπόστασις and οὐσία is "existence; for it is, or in other words, exists[1]".

The Creeds devised as substitutes for the Creed of Nicaea are usually content to forbid the use of οὐσία without mention of ὑπόστασις, but the Synod of Constantinople in 360 which concluded the Homoean compromise declared against ὑπόστασις too—evidently regarding the words as synonymous (*v.* the Creed in Hahn³, p. 209)[2].

It was at the Synod of Alexandria in 362, presided over by Athanasius, that formal recognition was first conceded to the usage of the word ὑπόστασις which made it possible to speak of the Trinity as τρεῖς ὑποστάσεις, while still being faithful to the definitions of the doctrine at Nicaea. But at the same time the older and original usage, according to which μία ὑπόστασις only could be said, and τρεῖς ὑποστάσεις was tritheistic, received like recognition. Athanasius questioned those who were blamed for saying τρεῖς ὑποστάσεις and those who were blamed for saying μία ὑπόστασις, and found that the representatives of both usages agreed in the Nicene doctrine and in anathematising Arius, Sabellius, and Paul of Samosata, and that they all said that in future they would prefer to be content to use the language of the Nicene Creed (Ath. *ad Antiochenos*, §§ 5, 6)[3].

[1] So Hilary *de Syn.* 84 (Hahn³ p. 162) quoting the Creed gives *vel ex alia substantia aut essentia* as the Latin equivalent, shewing that he realised no distinction between the words (no difference between *substantia* and *essentia* having ever been recognised, except that the former was of genuine Latin origin while the latter was its unsuccessful Greek competitor): while Lucifer *de non parcendo in Deum delinquentibus* (Migne *PL.* xiii 935 ff.) is content to write *vel ex alia substantia* only.

Dr Hatch *Hibbert Lectures* p. 276 (one of the Lectures not revised by himself), and Mr Ottley *Doctrine of the Incarnation* vol. ii p. 256 after him, quote Ath. *Dial. de Trin.* i 2 and Ath. et Cyril. *in expos. orthod. fid.* to shew that Athanasius used ὑπόστασις in the sense of 'person'. But the former writing is certainly later than 381, and is printed by Migne among the 'spurious' works attributed to Athanasius. The latter I cannot identify, unless it is the Athanasian exposition of the Creed given in Migne vol. xxvi p. 1231 (found in a Vatican MS of Cyril's works), in which ὑπόστασις is the equivalent of οὐσία.

[2] So, for example, Cyril of Jerusalem regularly uses ὑπόστασις and not οὐσία (ἡ ὑπόστασις ἡ θεία *Cat.* vi 5, ἡ πονηρὰ ὑπόστασις *ib.* 13, πρὸ πάσης ὑποστάσεως *ib.* vii 5, ὑπόστασις οὐρανοῦ *ib.* ix 5)—contrasted with φύσις *ib.* xvi 24 (the catechumen need not be anxious to enquire about the φύσις or the ὑπόστασις of the Spirit, but may be content to know that there is Father, Son, and Spirit), and in the same sense *ib.* xvi 5, xvii 17.

[3] Socrates *H. E.* iii 7 says it was determined that such expressions as οὐσία and ὑπόστασις ought not to be used in reference to God, but that in refutation of

Yet so many 'orthodox' theologians had become accustomed to the expression *τρεῖς ὑποστάσεις*, and it was so obviously useful, that the conciliatory agreement which was reached by those who were present at this synod could not be expected to be permanent; and ultimately the two terms *οὐσία* and *ὑπόστασις* passed together into Catholic use to express respectively the one Godhead and the forms of its existence:— *οὐσία* the existence or essence or substantial entity of the Trinity as God; *ὑπόστασις* the existence in a particular mode, the manner of being of each of the 'Persons'.

More than any others the Cappadocian Fathers, and Basil perhaps in particular, contributed to securing currency for this distinction. But another Cappadocian, of less untarnished reputation, was among the first to note and describe this Eastern terminology.

One of the clearest definitions of the limited sense of *ὑπόστασις* is given by Basil of Ancyra in the statement explanatory of *ὅμοιον κατὰ πάντα* which he drew up after accepting the Dated Creed (359). He has declared that the phrase *κατὰ πάντα* necessarily means much more than Arians profess. It means that the Son is like *οὐ κατὰ τὴν βούλησιν καὶ τὴν ἐνέργειαν μόνην...ἀλλὰ κατὰ τὴν ὕπαρξιν καὶ κατὰ τὴν ὑπόστασιν καὶ κατὰ τὸ εἶναι ὡς υἱός*....And then he proceeds: *καὶ μὴ ταρασσέτω τὸ τῶν ὑποστάσεων ὄνομά τινας. διὰ τοῦτο γὰρ ὑποστάσεις οἱ ἀνατολικοὶ λέγουσιν, ἵνα τὰς ἰδιότητας τῶν προσώπων ὑφεστώσας καὶ ὑπαρχούσας γνωρίσωσιν. εἰ γὰρ πνεῦμα ὁ πατήρ, πνεῦμα καὶ ὁ υἱός, πνεῦμα καὶ τὸ ἅγιον πνεῦμα, οὐ νοεῖται πατὴρ ὁ υἱός. ὑφέστηκε δὲ καὶ τὸ πνεῦμα, ὃ οὐ νοεῖται υἱός, ὃ καὶ οὐκ ἔστι (τὸ πνεῦμα οὐ νοεῖται υἱός, ὑφέστηκε δὲ καὶ τὸ πνεῦμα τὸ ἅγιον)—καὶ οὐκέτι τὸ πνεῦμα τὸ ἅγιον, οὐδὲ ὁ πατήρ, οὐδὲ ὁ υἱός, ἀλλὰ πνεῦμα ἅγιον ἐκ πατρὸς δι' υἱοῦ πιστοῖς διδόμενον—εἰκότως ὑφεστῶτος καὶ ὑπάρχοντος πατρὸς καὶ υἱοῦ καὶ τοῦ πνεύματος τοῦ ἁγίου, τὰς ἰδιότητας—ὡς προειρήκαμεν—προσώπων ὑφεστώτων ὑποστάσεις ὀνομάζουσιν οἱ ἀνατολικοί, οὐχὶ τὰς τρεῖς ὑποστάσεις τρεῖς ἀρχὰς ἢ τρεῖς θεοὺς λέγοντες....ὁμολογοῦσι γὰρ μίαν εἶναι θεότητα ἐμπεριέχουσαν δι' υἱοῦ ἐν πνεύματι ἁγίῳ τὰ πάντα...ὅμως τὰ πρόσωπα ἐν ταῖς ἰδιότησι τῶν ὑποστάσεων εὐσεβῶς γνωρίζουσι, τὸν πατέρα ἐν τῇ πατρικῇ αὐθεντίᾳ ὑφεστῶτα νοοῦντες, καὶ τὸν υἱὸν οὐ μέρος ὄντα τοῦ πατρὸς ἀλλὰ καθαρῶς ἐκ πατρὸς τέλειον ἐκ τελείου γεγεννημένον καὶ ὑφεστῶτα ὁμολογοῦντες, καὶ τὸ πνεῦμα τὸ ἅγιον...ἐκ πατρὸς δι' υἱοῦ ὑφεστῶτα γνωρίζοντες.* (Epiph. *adv. Haer.* LXXIII 16, 17.)

Sabellian error they were admissible, so that each of the Trinity might be recognised as God in his own *ὑπόστασις*, and we might not—through poverty of language—account as one thing that which was threefold in designation.

The first phrase, that the Son is like *κατὰ τὴν ὑπόστασιν*, must no doubt be interpreted in a somewhat wider sense of *ὑπόστασις* (more as *οὐσία*), but when he sets himself to explain the exact significance of the word as the Easterns employed it, he gives it the meaning of Basil of Caesarea's *τρόπος ὑπάρξεως* (cf. also Greg. Nyss. *Or. Cat.* ch. iv.).

In like manner Basil of Caesarea clearly defines the sense of *ὑπόστασις* as *τὸ ἰδίως λεγόμενον*. It is a limitation—a separation of certain circumscribed conceptions from the general idea. "Not the "indefinite conception of *οὐσία*, which, because what is signified is "common to all, finds no fixity, but that which by means of the special "characteristics (or properties) which are made apparent gives fixity "and circumscription to that which is common and uncircumscribed[1]."

And again (*Ep.* 214) "*οὐσία* has the same relation to *ὑπόστασις* as "the common has to the particular. Every one of us both shares in "existence by the common term of *οὐσία* and by his own properties is "such or such an one. In the same manner, in the matter in question, "the term *οὐσία* is common, like goodness or Godhead or any similar "attribute (i.e. *it* is not 'goodness' or any attribute); while *ὑπόστασις* "is contemplated in the special property of Fatherhood, Sonship, or the "power to sanctify (sc. is the particular mode of existence)[2]."

There is thus *μία οὐσία* and *τρεῖς ὑποστάσεις*, or *μία οὐσία ἐν τρισὶν ὑποστάσεσιν*—one substance or essence in three subsistencies, or forms or modes or spheres of existence: one God permanently existing in three eternal modes. The *οὐσία* of Father and Son and Holy Spirit is one and the same. Both Father and Son together with the Holy Spirit are the Godhead. The one Being exists in three forms or spheres. The one God is tri-personal.

This is exactly what *ὁμοούσιος* as regards the Son meant to the Nicenes, and exactly what *ὁμοιούσιος* does not mean. 'Man' is *οὐσία*: a particular man, e.g. Paul, is *ὑπόστασις* (but see the warnings as to the limits to the analogy between 'man' and 'God'). So 'God' is *οὐσία*: but closer definition of the mode of his existence as Father, Son, and Holy Spirit is *ὑπόστασις*.

[1] *Ὁ γὰρ ἄνθρωπον εἰπὼν ἐσκεδασμένην τινὰ διάνοιαν τῷ ἀορίστῳ τῆς σημασίας τῇ ἀκοῇ ἐνεποίησεν· ὥστε τὴν μὲν φύσιν ἐκ τοῦ ὀνόματος δηλωθῆναι, τὸ δὲ ὑφεστὸς καὶ δηλούμενον ἰδίως ὑπὸ τοῦ ὀνόματος πρᾶγμα μὴ σημανθῆναι. Ὁ δὲ Παῦλον εἰπὼν ἔδειξεν ἐν τῷ δηλουμένῳ ὑπὸ τοῦ ὀνόματος πράγματι ὑφεστῶσαν τὴν φύσιν. τοῦτο οὖν ἐστιν ἡ ὑπόστασις, οὐχ ἡ ἀόριστος τῆς οὐσίας ἔννοια, μηδεμίαν ἐκ τῆς κοινότητος τοῦ σημαινομένου στάσιν εὑρίσκουσα, ἀλλ' ἡ τὸ κοινόν τε καὶ ἀπερίγραπτον ἐν τῷ τινὶ πράγματι διὰ τῶν ἐπιφαινομένων ἰδιωμάτων παριστῶσα καὶ περιγράφουσα.* (*Ep.* 38. 3.)

[2] Cf. also *Epp.* 125, 236.

(4) τὸ ὑποκείμενον.

The usage of τὸ ὑποκείμενον is declared by Aristotle in the words μάλιστα δοκεῖ εἶναι οὐσία τὸ ὑποκείμενον τὸ πρῶτον. (*Met.* vi 3. 1.)

Bonitz gives instances of three closely related uses:

(1) of the ὕλη which is determined by 'form',

(2) of the οὐσία in which πάθη, συμβεβηκότα inhere,

(3) of the subject to which predicates are referred.

But since ὕλη itself is referred to the notion of οὐσία, the uses (1) and (2) are not rigidly distinguished; and since εἶναι (ὑπάρχειν) and λέγεσθαι (κατηγορεῖσθαι) are closely connected, the uses (2) and (3) are not rigidly distinguished.

On the whole, the ordinary use of the term is of the underlying something (the *substratum*) to which (as to οὐσία) are logically opposed all affections and accidents (πάθη, συμβεβηκότα), and the term is regularly used by the Cappadocian theologians as applied to the Divine Being to express that which underlies it, so to say, and makes it what it is.

But it would not be exact to say that in the writings of careful theologians τὸ ὑποκείμενον is ever precisely the equivalent of οὐσία[1]. It probably always conveys a slightly different sense. It is at all events οὐσία regarded from a special point of view. And hence it follows that it may be used, without violation of its proper sense, to express that which constitutes individual existence; and so on occasion Origen used it, as we have seen, and after him Basil at all events, and Gregory of Nyssa. E.g. Basil *Ep.* ix 2 says of Dionysius of Alexandria that for the purpose of opposing the impiety of Sabellius it would have been enough if he had pointed out that the Father and the Son are not identical as to their existence or *substratum* (οὐ ταὐτὸν τῷ ὑποκειμένῳ), and had thus 'scored' against the blasphemer: but that he was not satisfied with laying down a difference of 'hypostases', but must needs go further, in order to win a superabundant victory, and assert also difference of 'substance'—so falling himself into the opposite error. Here clearly Basil means by τὸ ὑποκείμενον that which constitutes

[1] In the passage cited *supra* p. 57 from Greg. Nyss. *Or. Cat.* 3 some MSS read τῇ φύσει and some τῇ οὐσίᾳ for τῷ ὑποκειμένῳ. Krabinger notes that the variants are mere glosses. It would be more exact to say that they shew that the general sense of the passage was caught, but that accurate discrimination was wanting.

Τὸ ὑποκείμενον is used in the same sense in Greg. Nyss. *Or. Cat.* Prol. (Krabinger p. 4 l. 34), and § 5 (K. p. 13 l. 3) and in the *contra Eunom.*

individual existence. To assert a difference of οὐσία is going further than to maintain a difference as to τὸ ὑποκείμενον. And cf. Greg. Nyss. *Or. Cat.*: see *supra* p. 57 note.

Cotelier's 'Harlaean' MSS.

The correspondence between Basil and Apollinarius referred to *supra* pp. 38—45 was printed by Cotelier 'ex Harlaeano MS', and the source of other documents which he edited was indicated by the same or a similar description. What these 'Harlaean' MSS were is not quite clear, but in all probability they belonged to the library of Achille de Harlay (1581—1646), who was bishop of St Malo and well known as a patron of learning and a collector of Hebrew, Arabic, Chaldee, and Syriac MSS. [The collection of Robert Harley (1661—1724), Earl of Oxford, seems to have been made for the most part at all events after the year 1700.]